How to WIN at the Game of FINANCES

SHAWN MILLER

DEDICATION

I dedicate this book to my parents who taught me the importance of saving and investing.

ACKNOWLEDGEMENT

I would like to express my gratitude to the many people who have helped make this book possible. Thank you to those who helped with numerous hours of editing. Thank you for those who encouraged, supported, and assisted in this undertaking.

CONTENTS

1

INTRODUCTION

Are you ready to be DEBT FREE? You can be. In fact, not only can you be debt free, you can have money left over to INVEST. This book can completely change your life. Are you ready? Are you sure? If you are not ready, simply put down this book. I am kidding. You are ready. You are beyond ready. Today is the beginning of a new chapter in your life. Remember this day. It is the day you began the goal toward being debt free and being able to invest.

Think of today as the first day of the new season. Last year is behind us. The failures and fumbles from last year are forgotten. Today is the first day of practice. What you do from this day forward will determine the outcome at the end of the season. You can have another losing season, or you can win the championship game. It is completely up to you. As the coach, I want you to win. But no matter how much I want you to win, I cannot make you win. You have to want to win. You have the ability to win, if you have the desire. I see something in you that you do not see in yourself. You are a winner. And you can win at the game of finances. Are you ready?

Before we begin, I need you to know that this stuff really does work. It has worked in my family, and it will work for you as well. I want you to win. And YOU CAN. All you need to do is follow the steps. If you do, you will experience the freedom and rewards of having no debt and have savings for your future. You just finished chapter 1. See, this isn't so hard.

2

THE PLAYBOOK

When I was going to college at the University of Texas at Austin I got a job as a tutor. My job was to tutor the athletes, so that they could pass their classes and focus on the sport they were playing. One of the athletes I tutored was the starting quarterback of the football team. He and I would talk about economics during the week, and then he would go to football practice to work on the plays for the game. The Longhorns went on to win most of their games while I was a student there under their relatively new coach Mac Brown. It was exciting to be at the game where running back Ricky Williams broke the NCAA all-time rushing yards record and then went on to win the Heisman trophy.

The Longhorns were successful because they had a great coach, great players, and great plays. But I wonder, how successful the team would had been if coach Mac Brown said, "We are not going to have any plays. I just want you guys to try your best, and we will see what happens." In other words the team is just going to make up plays as they go. They are not going to have a playbook or do any preplanning. Do you think they would have won a national championship? Do you think they would have won many games? Probably not. Even with great players and a great coach, a team is not going to win very many games without a playbook.

Just like it would be ridiculous for a coach to have no plays, it would be ridiculous for a business to have no plan or budget in place. Imagine if a corporation thought that way. What if Exxon just winged it? What if Apple just spent money without any plan? How long would they remain one of the largest companies in the world? The answer is not that long. You see, all of these companies need a plan to be successful. Investors would agree that a corporation is mismanaged if they had no financial plan.

The same is true with you and I. We need a spending plan to be successful in our finances. We might be able to wing it for a while, but in the long run, we will not win many games, remain "in business," or reach our full potential without a plan.

Having a financial plan will help our money from simply disappearing. Money is like fire. It has power, but it must be controlled and directed. Without direction it will burn out of control and quickly. A fire that is out of control can burn down an entire home and destroy everything a family owns. However, a fire that is under control can provide many benefits to a family such as heating the home, cooking a meal, and providing hot water.

Rick Warren, author of the bestselling book *Purpose Driven Life*, says we need a budget because "Our yearnings exceed our earnings." What he means is that our desires will always be greater than our income. Whether we have a hundred dollars or a hundred million, we can always find more ways to spend our money than there is money available.

What if I told you that you can have a million dollars? What would you do with it? Buy a new house? A car? A vacation? Help others? Save some? Most people have imagined what they would do if they faced this "difficult" decision. The reality is that most people will earn over a million dollars over their lifetime. So the real question is not what would you do, but what WILL you do?

What you need to do is have a plan Stan. You need to know in advance what you are going to do. The plan is called a budget. Now, I know that the word budget sounds like a four letter word to some people, so how about calling it a spending plan instead.[1] You need a spending plan for all of your money. You probably already have a spending plan in your head that tells you that you can't go and buy certain things (like a new Lamborghini) this week, but you do have enough money to afford other things. What we need to do is take what is in your head and put it on paper to make it official. We need to create your playbook.

There are many benefits to having a spending plan. Having a plan will help your money go further. You will be able to do more with your money. Think of money like gasoline. You can fill a racecar with gas, and the motor will use the gas to make the racecar go. However, if you add fuel injection or a turbocharger, that same gas will make the racecar have much more power. You will be able to race even faster. You see, gas mixed with air under pressure creates a more powerful engine. The same is true with money. Money that is mixed with the pressure of a budget is more powerful than money that simply leaks out of our wallet.

In addition to being more effective, spending plans increase the peace in your family. One of the top causes of divorce in America is money fights. Couples fight because there is no plan in place on how to spend the family's money. This is an unnecessary stress that can be resolved by simply having a spending plan.

If spending plans are so important, and they can help us make our money go further, why doesn't everyone have a spending plan? The answer varies. Some people mistakenly believe that having one will mean they can never do anything fun ever again. This is not the case. A financial plan can, and should, include money for fun. In fact you can put as much "fun money" into your plan as you want. It is YOUR PLAN, and you get to decide how you are going to spend YOUR MONEY.

Others don't have a budget because they believe it is too much work, or that they are not organized enough to keep track of everything. I am not going to lie and say it isn't any work, but there are ways to make having a spending plan very easy. We will get into that later, but for now, all we need to realize is that the benefit of having a plan is so much better than the stress of dealing with money problems.

Also, there are those who do not want to create a spending plan because they are afraid of what they will find. They know that there will have to be some changes in their life, and they really don't want to change, and they don't want to have to be accountable to anyone including themselves. The reality is that change is difficult; however, even the smallest of changes can lead to drastic increases in your quality of life.

What if I am a millionaire already? Do I still need a budget or spending plan? The answer is a resounding yes. One of my prior jobs involved being the CPA for the wealthiest family that lived in the city where I resided in southern California. This man was a doctor, his wife was a doctor, and they owned the hospital where they worked. I helped oversee his many assets, properties, and millions that he made each year. Although this family made millions, they also spent millions. In fact, he was in financial trouble because he spent more than he made. It doesn't seem possible, but it can happen to anyone.

There are many wealthy people who have mismanaged their money and ended up having to file for bankruptcy. The 80's singer MC Hammer who sang "Too Legit to Quit" had to file bankruptcy on $13.7 million worth of debt. His overspending on a 30 million dollar mansion and paying people a total of $500,000 a month to work for him finally led to bankruptcy.

Another example is the boxer Mike Tyson who has reportedly earned over $400 million during his boxing career. Despite all of this money he still had to file bankruptcy on $27 million of debt.[2] Part of the problem was his lavish lifestyle which cost about $400,000 a month to maintain.

So, you can see that you can make millions each year, and still have money problems. Being a millionaire does not make money problems go away. In other words, there is never going to come a point where you can say, "I can buy everything and still have money left over." Even millionaires know there are certain things they cannot afford. And even billionaires know there are certain things they cannot afford.

That is why I like to say, "It doesn't matter how much you

make. What matters is how much you spend." You can make millions and still be in debt, and you can make minimum wage and be debt free. Your SPENDING has more to do with your financial situation than your income does. However, we focus much of our time on how we can bring in more money and very little time on the money that is going out. That is why you need a plan.

Having a plan is no different than being on a diet. When someone is on a diet, they will try to consume less calories than they burn in a day. The same is true with a financial plan. The goal is to SPEND LESS THAN YOU MAKE. It is just that simple. The hardest part is dealing with us. We get in the way of our own success. As your financial coach, I need to tell you something very important. Stop it. I want you to be a success. Your family would like for you to be successful in your finances. If you want to win at this game, I need you to be ALL IN. It may be difficult at times, and you may want to quit or give up, but YOU CAN DO THIS. I believe in you. You have the ability to be financially successful. Let's get started and put together your plan.

At the back of this book, in Appendix A, I have a plan that you can use. The plan is divided into eight different plays or sections. Simply fill it out based on what you've spent in prior months. This plan is your first step toward winning the game of finance in your life. Let's do this.

Once you have completed your spending plan, you will want to keep track of your spending each month. In the electronic age many people want something digital to keep track of their spending. The good news is that there are many apps available to help you do just that. One of the apps that I have used in the past is called Mint. This financial app will allow you to track all of your spending in an easy to use format. You can connect your checking account to the app and download your transactions, so that you do not have to spend your time entering information. This is a great way to see what you are spending on each of the categories of your budget. Most people do not realize how much they spend on going out to eat, entertainment, and groceries. This app helps you to easily find out how much you spend and where.

This app also helps you stick to your budget once you have one in place. You can enter your budget into the app, and then as you spend money, the transactions are automatically downloaded and categorized. You can check the app each day to see how much of your coffee budget is left, or how much fun money you have left to spend. You can also have notifications sent to you when you get close to being over budget in a certain category. .

Whatever app you decide to use, or if you decide to keep track of everything on a spreadsheet or a piece of paper, find something that will work for you. Remember the goal is to help you. You don't have to use the fanciest tool if a simple one will work better for you.

Individual or Joint Accounts

I am often asked if married couples should have two individual accounts or one joint account for their main checking account(s). In other words should their money be in one pile that they both spend from, or should each person have their own pile that they control? I believe that the number of checking accounts doesn't really matter. What matters is that ALL of the money is being spent as part of ONE plan. In other words, it is not a good idea for a couple to say this is "my" money and that is "your" money. All of the money should be seen as "our" money. Now you may decide as a couple that one account is going to pay this bill and that bill, and the other account is going to pay the other bills. However, this should be discussed as a couple and incorporated as part of the family budget.

My wife and I have always had one joint checking account for paying bills. There have been times where she had a checking account for her businesses, but for us it made more sense to have one account for our main account. (I do understand that some people are spenders, and they probably would do better with a separate account to keep them from spending all of the money that the family earns). That is why this is a family decision, and there is no right or wrong answer, as long as the couple can use their decision to improve the financial situation in their home.

So let's get your playbook put together, so you can stop calling plays without a plan. Looking back you will be so glad that you have a plan in place, and your family will be grateful as well. It is time to win.

Questions for Study

1. Why doesn't everyone have a budget or spending plan?

2. Why is it important for you to have a budget or spending plan?

3. Why is getting started sometimes the hardest step in making a change in your life?

3

THE TRICK PLAY

I was at the dentist one day for a routine checkup. As I sat down in the chair, I noticed that the dentist office had installed some new televisions, so I could watch something while they cleaned my teeth. One of the college bowl games was playing, and I like college football. So, I was delighted to sit back for however long it took to get a cleaning.

As I was watching the game, and saw Boise State, I thought about the trick play that Boise State did back in the 2007 Fiesta Bowl. The play is called the Statue of Liberty, which is where the quarterback pretends to throw the ball, then stands like the Statue of Liberty with his hand in the air with the ball behind his back. This play allowed Boise State to win the game in 2007, and is still one of the greatest plays in college football.

As I sat in the dentist chair enjoying the game, Boise State did that same play that they are now famous for. I nearly jumped out of the chair when I saw the play. I was so excited, that I asked the hygienist to watch the replay because it was such an iconic play. Boise State went on to win the game, just like they did before, using the same trick play–the Statue of Liberty.

Football teams use a trick play when they have exhausted all of their normal plays. They save the trick play for an emergency situation. Either they need to score some points because time is running out, or they are in need of a momentum shift.

In the same way, you need a trick play for your finances. You need a play that you can run when an emergency takes place. That trick play is called an emergency fund. In other words, you need some money set aside for the unexpected. When your car won't start and you need to rush out and fix it, your emergency fund will provide you with the money you need to take care of the situation.

Most people do not have an emergency fund. So what do you think they do when that emergency takes place in their life? That's right. They put it on the credit card. There is only one problem with that. They have to pay that money back with interest (and usually it is at a very high interest rate).

That is why having an emergency fund will help remove

stress from your life. When most people have a financial emergency, two things normally happen. First, they get upset because of the emergency (the car broke down). Second, they get upset because they have to figure out how to pay for the emergency (repairing the car).

The good news is that when you have your emergency fund in place, you only have the stress of the car breaking down without the stress of how to pay for the repair. Your stress will be cut in half! Also, the emergency won't cost you as much because you won't have to pay interest like those who used a credit card (You may have even earned some interest from having your emergency fund in a savings account).

So how much should you have tucked away for emergencies? How about $500–$1,000. Save this amount in an account for those emergencies that happen in life. Now remember that an emergency is not seeing a new movie that is playing on Friday. It's also not going out to a fancy dinner because there is nothing good to eat at the house. An emergency fund is for emergencies.

Since it is for emergencies, I recommend that people keep their emergency fund at a separate bank from their checking account. That way you won't be tempted to make a transfer from your emergency fund when you log into your online banking. It should be somewhat inconvenient to get to, so you are not tempted to spend it for non-emergencies. However, it should not be so hard to get to that you have to sell stocks or bonds just to get the money for the emergency. In other words, just leave it in a savings account that is at a bank where you can make an online transfer or walk into the bank if there is a real emergency, and you need the money. The point of this money is to be a safety net when something happens. It is not an investment where you are trying to get the highest return possible (We will talk about investing other money in another chapter).

Your emergency fund is one of the most important things you can do to help your finances. It is so important that I recommend you get your emergency fund in place before you even start worrying about your credit cards, your 401K, or investing in the stock market. It doesn't do you any good to begin paying off your credit cards without an emergency fund because you need the emergency fund to keep you from having to use the credit card for emergencies. Make the emergency fund your priority, and you will be one step closer to reaching your financial goals.

Setting up an emergency fund is a small step in the grand scheme of finance. However, it is a big step for most people. This is the first step in saying, "I am going to make a change." It is like when someone decides to lose weight. The hardest part sometimes is just getting started. Taking the first step is sometimes harder than taking the next 99 steps. The same is true in your finances. Saving some money for emergencies sounds easy, but doing it can be challenging. So, let me remind you of something very important. YOU CAN DO THIS. That's right. You can do something new and begin a savings account for emergencies. You can have your trick play ready for when life throws you a curve ball. And when life happens, you will be able to hit the ball, run the touchdown, score the goal, and win the game. Now go get started, and set up an emergency fund.

Questions for Study

1. What is the best way to keep from paying for emergencies with a credit card?

2. Why doesn't everyone have an emergency fund?

3. What is one change you can make today, so that you can begin saving toward your emergency fund?

4

NFL PLAYERS IN HIGH SCHOOL

I have spent over a two decades living in Texas. This state is known for several things, one of which is high school football. The local high school where I live has won numerous state championships and have made it to the playoffs every year that I have followed them. The last game I went to they were winning 40-0! And it was only half time! They are a great football team, and they lose very few games.

Now let's say one of high school's rivals decided to make it their goal to beat the local team. The head coach of this rival team decides he is going to hire an NFL quarterback to lead the team to victory. Besides being illegal, this would be a bad decision for the high school football coach. NFL quarterbacks are very expensive to hire, and it would cost the school millions of dollars to hire someone with that level of talent. The only way the high school would be able to afford this player is by taking out a loan and financing the quarterback's salary.

Even if the high school and football league approved the deal, it would be a bad idea for the school. After a couple years the high school would have a mountain of debt, and nothing but a trophy to show for all the money that was spent.

The same is true in our personal finances. As coaches of our money we should not get into debt by using credit cards. Credit cards have become the staple of American financing, and the average household has over $15,000 in credit card debt.[1] Now let's say the average family is paying their monthly payment on their credit cards, and they run into a difficult month and are late on making their payment. The bank usually decides to increase their interest rate to 29.99%. At this point they continue to make large monthly payments ($400 per month). However, even at four hundred dollars a month, it will take them 10 years to get out of debt! And by the time they are done paying the debt off, that $15,000 worth of stuff they bought has actually cost them $48,000! They paid three times the actual cost, and it took 10 years to pay it off.

For this and many other reasons, I do not recommend families use credit cards. Now over the years of speaking at conferences on finance, I will get couples that say to me, "but what about the points we earn on our credit cards?"

Now let's step back for a second and think about this. Do

the credit card companies like you? No. Do they want to give you something for nothing? No. Why do they give you 1% cash back or airline miles? Because they are charging you 18-29% interest. And even if you are one of those savvy people that pay off your credit card each month to avoid interest and get the miles, what happens if you mess up just one month because you had an emergency happen in your life? You end up paying the high interest rate, which costs you more than your miles for the entire year.

That is why it is better to forgo the miles and pay using cash or your debit card. Credit card companies have structured credit cards to keep you in debt. They only make money when you have debt. So their job is to keep you in debt. That is why the minimum payment is always so low. It is designed that way, so that you will not get out of debt for a very long time.

So the goal should be to not use credit cards. Never. I currently have one credit card. It sits in my wallet and collects dust. I keep a zero balance on it, and only use it if my debit card malfunctions. It really is just a line of credit that I have available to me that serves as the backup to my emergency fund.

Building Credit

Other people have asked me, "But what about building

up credit? We have bad credit, or no credit, and need to build up credit." First of all, if you have a car that you make payments on, you are building credit. Secondly, you can get one credit card, and put one utility bill on there each month, and then pay it off at the end of each month. For example, you can put your cell phone bill on the credit card, and then pay off the card at the end of the month. By doing this you build your credit.

Some people think that they have to have debt to build credit. That is not true. The credit score companies give you a score based on your risk of default. If you are paying your credit card on time each month, it shows the credit companies that you are responsible and will pay all of your debt on time. That is what they are looking for, not how much debt you can accumulate. They want to know how good are you at making your monthly payments on time.

You may be thinking, "Ok, I won't use credit cards in the future. But right now I already have a lot of debt. What do I do?" If this is you, then you need to run a special play called "double team, and man to man." The way this play works is you need to get a list of all of your credit cards and the balance on each card (Appendix B). You then pay the minimum payment on each card (man to man) except for the card with the lowest balance. For this card you are going to double team, or double pay the minimum payment. By doubling (or tripling if you can) the minimum payment you are going to pay off this card quickly. Once you get the first card paid off, you are going to take the payment you were making on the first card and use it to pay the second card (on top of the minimum payment you were already making).

Once the second card is paid off, you can take the payments you were making on the first two cards, and now make them to the third card. You continue this until all of the credit cards are paid off.

Another way of looking at this is that you are paying the same amount each month toward your debt, even though the minimum payments will begin to go down. If you run the double team, and man to man play on your credit cards you will eventually have NO CREDIT CARD DEBT. How would that make you feel. No credit cards. Let it sink in for a moment. Would you feel less stress and more relaxed? Of course you would. It is a great feeling, and one you should pursue.

Now the reality is that if you have a large amount of credit card debt, you probably did not get into debt overnight. So just like you don't get into debt overnight, you also don't get out of debt overnight. It takes time. It takes giving up a few things in the short run, so that you can save thousands in interest in the long run.

Sometimes I have people ask me about the order of

paying off their credit cards. They say that mathematically it would be better to pay off the highest interest rate credit card first, instead of the lowest balance credit card. Mathematically they are correct. But this is not about math. If they were focused on math, they would not be in this situation in the first place. This is about motivation. When a couple pays off a credit card, even if it only has a balance of a couple hundred dollars, they have a victory. And when you get a victory, you will be motivated to get another credit card paid off to achieve another victory. In football, many coaches schedule a couple easy teams to play in the beginning of the year. They do this to build up the team's confidence. It is much easier to face a tough team knowing that you have won in the past, than it is if you have never won. The same is true in your finances.

The goal is for you and your family to be credit card debt free. You will feel so much better without debt. There is a proverb that says, "The rich rule over the poor, and the borrower is slave to the lender."[2] Nobody wants to be a slave; however, debt does create a slave-like relationship, where one person is tied to a bank or institution until their debt is paid in full. Let's break the chains of bondage and be debt free! Today can be the beginning of a new chapter in your life.

Debt Consolidation

Many people ask me what I think about debt consolidation. For example, a family may have several credit cards, medical bills, and other debt, and they would like to consolidate it into one payment and hopefully at a lower interest rate.

On the surface debt consolidation sounds like a great idea. Lower interest rate and lower payment. Then what is the catch? The problem with debt consolidation is that the amount of time to pay off the loan increases. Increasing the amount of time of the loan, means that you also increase the amount of interest you end of paying for your debt.

For example, let's say that you have $25,000 in credit card debt. One card has $10,000 at 11% and will take 3 years to pay off. The second card has a $15,000 balance at 12% and will take 4 years to pay off. Let's say that your monthly payments on the first loan is $327.39, and the payment on the second load is $395.01. So your total credit card payment is $722.44.

You apply for a loan consolidation, and they tell you that your new interest rate will be 9%, and your monthly payment will be $402.23. That means your monthly payment will go down $320.17 per month, and your interest rate will go down 2-3%. That sounds like a great deal. The problem is that instead of having both credit cards paid off in 4 years, now it will take you 7 years to pay them off. That means you will end up paying a total of $33,787.32. So your $25,000 debt has cost you $8,787.32 in interest. This is over $3,000 MORE in interest that you will have to pay because you got the loan consolidation. In other words, you would have saved more money by NOT consolidating your debt.

Furthermore, loan consolidation does not fix the issue that caused you to be in debt. Often times people find themselves in debt because of poor spending habits or lack of self-control in spending in certain areas. For example, someone could have a habit of spending too much money on clothes which causes them to fall into debt. Debt consolidation does not fix the underlying cause which created the debt. That is why it is normally better to focus on breaking spending habits and addressing overspending issues than it is to try debt consolidation.

Bankruptcy

When I was in high school I played four years of football. We had one of the worst football teams ever. My freshman year we lost every game. My sophomore year we lost every game. My junior year we lost every game. My senior year we finally won two games, and we were very excited. I still remember the last game of my senior year, where my school played the best team in California. That team was beating my school 50 to 0 at half time. It was embarrassing. I'm sure my coach would have liked to have traded all of his players that day for all new ones.

Some people feel the same way in their finances. They find themselves in so much debt that they feel like the only way out is to file bankruptcy and start over. Chapter 7 bankruptcy is the typical bankruptcy that people refer to when the say they went bankrupt. This form of bankruptcy allows you to "get a fresh start" and clear off your debts, so you can start over. It allows you to keep some assets, depending on your state. For example, in Texas you can keep up to $50,000 of personal property.[3] You can keep a certain amount of your retirement (401K, pension), and you can keep your home in most situations.

There is another form of bankruptcy, which is referred to a Chapter 13. This form of bankruptcy is also known as reorganization. This is where some debts are discharged, and others are restructured to make it easier to repay.

Should I File for Bankruptcy?

The real question is, "Should I file bankruptcy?" This is a difficult question because it really depends on an individual's situation. If you are able to repay your debts, it is always better to pay than to not pay. Remember, if you declare bankruptcy, someone is going to lose money. You may be free from the debt, but the person you owe is not going to get repaid. Sometimes we may think that these large companies have plenty of money, so they will be fine. That is not always the case. Sometimes large companies fail when people do not repay their debts. When the mortgage crises happened, many large banks failed because people did not pay their mortgages. In addition, small companies are impacted when debts are not repaid. The local furniture store or electronics store suffers when debts are not repaid.

When considering bankruptcy, you should also consider debts that you may have that cannot be forgiven. For example, you cannot go bankrupt on student loans. You also cannot go bankrupt on child support, alimony, IRS back taxes, and fines or penalties for breaking the law.

Although there are some limitations to bankruptcy, for some people this allows them to "reset" their financial situation and get back on their feet. Bankruptcy is a difficult decision, and one that should not be made lightly. However, it can be used in certain situations to overcome severe financial situations.

Questions for Study

1. What is the benefit of having no credit card debt?

2. The norm is to have credit card debt. What do you need to do differently in order to avoid having this kind of debt?

3. Should you have a balance on your credit card, so that you can build your credit?

5

THOUSAND DOLLAR SOCKS

Falke, a company in Germany, sells a pair of socks for $1,180, making them the most expensive socks in the world. These socks are made from Vicuna hair which is the most expensive fabric in the world. The Vicuna is an animal in Peru that resembles a lama. The wool from this animal is so delicate that it cannot be dyed. Therefore, you can only buy the sock in one color. Golden brown.

Now imagine a high school football coach spending his entire budget for the year so that each player can have a pair of these top of the line socks. However, once they buy these socks, they are not going to have any money left over for helmets, shoulder pads, and footballs. That would be ridiculous. How wise would this be? Besides being unwise, the coach would probably lose his job over it.

Even though it is easy to judge the coach for making an illogical decision, too often we make the same poor decisions in our finances. We buy the boat we cannot afford, or the purse that can only be purchased using our credit card, or whatever overpriced item we desire. We overspend and then stress that there isn't enough money for some basic items that we really do need.

So, instead of the coach buying the most expensive socks in the world, he should probably find ways to cut unnecessary costs and save some of his money.

One way to save money is to purchase items at a lower price. If you can get the exact same item cheaper at one store than another, it would make since to purchase it at the cheaper store (assuming the cost of shipping or driving is the same).

Although saving money by getting the best deal is great, the real question is, "Do you really need that item in the first place?" The answer to this question is often, "No, I don't need it, but I want it." I am not against you buying things you want. You can buy whatever you want with your money. The problem is when we buy things we can't afford, or we buy something, and then we get further into debt, and are not able to save. In other words, if you are out of debt, and you are saving money each month, then sure go out and buy as much useless stuff as you want. The problem is that most Americans are buying useless stuff they can't even afford.

So how do we overcome this way of thinking that has permeated our culture? First, we can avoid impulse buying. If we see something we really want, it might be helpful to wait a day or two. Just waiting a couple days may help us to realize that this item is something we don't necessarily want anymore.

Secondly, we can talk to our spouse (if we are married) about the purchase. Often times our spouse is able to help us decide if the purchase is right for the family at that point in time. There are times my wife will ask me about a purchase, and I may say let's hold off on that for now. Then there are other times I say that sounds good and agree with her about the purchase. And I do the same thing with her about my purchases.

We also need to consider our motive for purchasing the item. Are we buying it because we feel depressed, and we feel that this item will make us happier? Are we buying it because we feel like we deserve it because we work hard? Or are we buying it because it is something we need or will help others? Unfortunately the motive for buying most stuff is for selfish reasons. We want the pleasure that the stuff will give us. I am not against buying stuff. You can get some stuff. But just don't let your stuff get you.

Automobiles

What is your strategy for getting the best deal when purchasing a car? Is your strategy like the coach that spends all of his money on the players' socks? Most people ignore all factors and simply focus on the payment amount. You should be concerned about the payment, but there are many other factors you should consider when buying a car.

One of the biggest factors to consider is whether to buy a new or used car. New cars are great because they are new; however, a new car does not come without a high cost. For example, let's say you go to the dealership and purchase a brand new car for $29,873. You get in the car and drive off the parking lot and add one mile to the vehicle. The car is now worth $27,314. You just lost $2,559 by driving one mile!

You continue driving the car for a year and add on another 15,000 miles. Now the car is worth $24,186. After one year you have now lost $5,687. After two years the car will be worth $20,579, and after five years the car will be worth $12,069.[1] So in five years you will have lost about 60% of the car's value. That is a high price to pay for having a new car.

On the other hand let's say you buy the same car, but this time the car is used. It is two years old, so you purchase it for $20,579. Already you just saved $9,294 off the original price. In addition the car will still be under the factory warranty, so if there are any problems, you can simply take it to the dealership to get fixed. Furthermore, after driving the vehicle for five years, your car is still worth about $10,000, which means you didn't lose as much value during the five years as you would have if the car had been new.

For this and other reasons, a used car is a great way to go if you want to save money. People that drive used cars are able to save more money and are able to get ahead in their finances without having to make a large sacrifice.

In the example we just looked at, we compared buying a new car to buying a car that was two years old. Some people are able to save even more money by purchasing a car that is even older, which allows them to pay cash instead of having car payments. Paying cash for an older car will free up your finances from having to make monthly payments (which include interest charges). This will allow you to save or get out of debt faster. Yes, you may have to make a few repairs if it is an older car, but even if you had to spend $100 a month on repairs, it would still be cheaper than a car payment.

For example, I paid cash for a vehicle last year. The vehicle cost me $2,000. Let's say the vehicle only lasts me one year and then completely stopped working. That means the vehicle only cost me $166 dollars a month. That is cheaper than any car payment. What if the car ends up lasting two years. Then it only cost me $83 dollars a month. That is very cheap. In addition to saving money on interest, you will save money on insurance. A new car will require you to have full coverage, and the cost will be high due to the high value of the new vehicle. A used car that you pay cash for only needs to have liability insurance since the vehicle doesn't have that much value.

I know that not everyone is willing to purchase a used car; however, it is a great way to save money. Another option you have if you decide to purchase a new car is to keep driving the vehicle even after it is paid off. This will allow you to save the payments you were making while continuing to get the benefit of driving the vehicle. I did this with one of the vehicles that I owned. I paid it off in three years, and then I continued driving it. I drove it, and drove it, and drove it. I ended up being able to use the vehicle for fourteen years, which meant that I had eleven years without a car payment!

Purchasing Vehicles

Purchasing a vehicle can be an exciting experience. However, it can also be an experience where you end up spending more than you were planning to spend. When you arrive at a dealership to purchase a vehicle, one of the first things they will ask you is whether you will be trading in a vehicle. It is better to say that you aren't sure yet. If you tell them you are going to trade in your old car, they will factor in the price of the new car with the value they plan on giving you for your old car in the price. Here is the problem. The way they finagle the price you often end up getting little to nothing for your old car.

If you have an old car to trade in it is better to wait until you finalize a price on the newer car before you haggle on the trade in. An even better option is to sell the used vehicle yourself. You will always get more money this way. Whatever you decide to do with your old car, you should always look up the Kelley Blue Book value before you make a decision. You can find the value of your car through www.kbb.com. It would be a waste to trade in your used car for $1,000 if the private party value is $4,000. You would basically gain an extra $3,000 by selling it yourself.

When you purchase a vehicle, the dealership will also try selling you an extended warranty. All vehicles come with a standard warranty. For example, the standard warranty could be 36 months or 36,000 miles for most things, and 60 months or 60,000 miles for the major things like the engine and transmission. Most vehicles come with a standard warranty; however, the months and mileage may vary. In addition to the standard warranty you may be offered an extended warranty that will cover the vehicle for a certain number of additional months and miles.

On average an extended warranty costs about $1,214. However on average 55% of the people who purchase the extended warranty will never use it. Out of those who do use the warranty, the average repair cost is $837.[2] That means on average people who use the extended warranty end up losing over $375. And obviously those who didn't use the warranty lost the entire $1,214. For this reason most people recommend that the extended not be purchased. You would be better off putting $1,214 in a savings account in case something happened, and you need to make a repair.

Financing Vehicles

Another question the dealership will ask you is about financing. They will gladly lend you the money needed to purchase the vehicle. Your best option financially is to pay cash. By paying cash you end up paying zero dollars in interest. The next best option is to get financing from your bank or a lender that is not part of the dealership. By having your own financing you are able to go from one dealership to the next and know that you can qualify for financing. This speeds up the process for you.

Having your own financing also keeps you from getting any surprises at the dealership. A dealership may advertise a low interest rate for financing, and then say you don't qualify for that rate. At that point you have nothing to compare to, and you may accept the rate they offer you. However, if you already have financing from the bank or outside lender, you know going into the dealership what you are going to have to pay in interest and fees.

Leases

Sometimes people ask if it is better to purchase or lease a vehicle. The commercials always focus on the lease price because it is cheaper than the purchase price. So, to the novice consumer they will assume that the lease is a better deal because it costs less per month than if they purchase the vehicle. There are a few reasons why the lease price is less.

The first reason is because when you lease a vehicle you are really just renting a car. So, if you lease a car for four years, at the end of four years you have nothing. However, if you purchase the vehicle at the end of four years, you have a car that you own (if you finance for four years or less). The point is that you will own a car worth thousands of dollars instead of having nothing. You can always trade in your vehicle and buy a new one at that point, or you can continue driving the car you own and have no car payments.

The other downside of having a lease is there are strict requirements that you must adhere to when returning the vehicle. For example, you may be only allowed to drive a certain number of miles, and if you go over, you will be charged a certain amount per mile over. Or you could be charged for excessive wear and tear on the vehicle if the vehicle is not clean and maintained properly. (This is like drafting a NFL football player and promising that he won't get hurt while he plays for you.)

Also when you lease a vehicle, you are typically required to make a large down payment on the vehicle, or you may need to make a large payment when the vehicle is returned. This can be seen as a hidden cost because it is not reflected in the monthly lease cost.

In summary, you want to consider all the costs of owning the vehicle when deciding whether to purchase or lease a vehicle.

Car Buying Tips

Another car buying tip is don't fall in love with one car. If you have to have this one car with this one set of options, then you are fairly limited. It is better to have a few options in mind, so that you don't end up paying more than you really want to pay.

Also, when you purchase a car, it is better to negotiate the price of the car not the monthly payment. The dealership may try to focus on the monthly payments, but the more important factor is the price of the car. For example, if the dealer says that they will add a warranty for $40 dollars a month, that might not seem like too much money for a warranty. But, if the dealer is financing your car for 5 years, then the total cost of the warranty ends up being $2,400. If the warranty normally cost $1,200, you ended up paying twice as much because you only focused on the increase in your monthly payment instead of the increase in the purchase price.

Food

How much do you spend on food each month? Do you know? Most people do not know. They might have an amount in their mind, but the actual amount is usually higher than they think. Spending money on food is one of the areas in our life where we can spend as much or a little as we want. We can eat fine dining three times a day, or we can eat Top Ramen (which is disgusting in my opinion) and water every day. Most people spend somewhere in between these two extremes.

For example, there are some people that are extreme couponers and will find the best deals along with other creative ideas to save money. One such man is Jeffrey Stray, who put himself on a strict budget to prove that people can live on less than they think. His goal was to live on $1 a day for 100 days.[3]

Using his extreme methods, he not only was able to meet his goal, but he had an abundance of food left over which he donated to charity.

Now, I am not advocating that you live on such a meager amount. I am simply pointing out that we are probably spending more on food than we could be spending. Going out to eat is probably the biggest contributor to overspending on food. Making meals at home almost always provides you with better quality food at a lower cost. Although it may not be as convenient, it will help your budget and health.

I also want to be clear that I am not against going out to eat. I enjoy taking my wife and children to a restaurant. However, it might be a good idea to have a monthly food budget. That way you can decide how often to go out to eat based on how much is left in the food budget for the month.

Another way to save money on food is by using coupons or taking advantage of in store specials. My mother was an expert at this. She would match a coupon with the store special and get the item for next to nothing. I remember her showing me receipts where she bought hundreds of dollars' worth of groceries for a few bucks! In other words, she got a lot of free groceries.

I know that some of us do not like to use coupons or look at store specials because it takes too much time, or it can be a hassle. Other people don't like to use coupons because of pride, and they don't want to look poor or cheap by using them. However, taking advantage of these discounts can free up money that you can use in other areas of your life.

For example, my wife and I were at the grocery store last week, and we saw that the cereal was on sale for cheaper than we had ever seen it before. Most of the cereal was sold out, but we still managed to buy a few more boxes than we normally do because we knew our three children would eat it. I mentioned to my wife that if we had a coupon for this cereal, it would have been a really, really good deal. My wife talked to her coupon friend and discovered that she had done just that. She was able to get the cereal for $.13 a box and was able to buy so many boxes! I say all of this to say that it is possible to save money on groceries, and finding discounts can save you money.

Questions for Study

1. If you try to pay less for an item by waiting until it is on sale or using a coupon, does that mean you are cheap or wise?

2. What is the benefit of trying to find the best deal for the items you are going to purchase?

3. What can you do before you go to the dealership to be better prepared when buying large items such as automobiles?

6

DEFENSE WINS CHAMPIONSHIPS

Offense wins games. Defense wins championships. Your team can have a great offense, but if you don't have a defense, you find yourself losing games because the other team will outscore you. On the other hand if you have a great defense and can keep the other team from scoring, then all you need is an average offense that can score a few points, so that you can win the game.

A few years ago the Blackhawks won the Stanley Cup. This team led the Western Conference with the fewest goals allowed and the highest save percentage. In other words, they had the best defense. Also a few years ago the Golden State Warriors won the NBA title. They led the NBA in defensive efficiency during the regular season. They also held their opponents to an NBA low 47 percent effective field goal percentage.[1] Again, they won because they had a great defense. I could go on about the Broncos winning the Super Bowl, and Alabama winning the National Championship in college football. The common theme is having a good defense wins championships.

In our finances a good defense means saving money. Offense is making money. Defense is saving money. You must have a good defense in your finances if you want to win big. You can always push yourself to make more money, get a raise, earn a promotion, and get that bonus, but without a defense you will find yourself still losing. You need to really focus on saving if you want to win in your finances.

There are three reasons to save money. We discussed the first one earlier with the trick play. Remember everyone should have an emergency fund for those unexpected curve balls that life throws at you.

The second reason we need to save is for predictable needs. A wise coach knows that he is going to have to spend money at the end of the year for the awards ceremony, or the alumni dinner, or for recruiting during off season. These are costs that he knows will take place. The same is true in our families. We know that birthdays, anniversaries, holidays, and other things will happen each year. So we should save money throughout the year so that we aren't scrambling around at the last minute figuring out how to squeeze it on the credit card.

The third reason we should save is for future goals. Maybe you want to save for college for the kids or a family vacation. The best way to reach these goals is to plan ahead and save for them.

Some countries are very good at saving. People in Ireland save nearly 20% of their income.[2] In Japan people save about 16% of their income.[3] However in the US, adults under 35 have a saving rate of negative 2%.[4] It is negative because they spend everything they make and then put some more on the credit card.

Unfortunately America is not very good at saving. Even though we are the wealthiest country in the world, we are not the best at saving. The US population makes up only 5% of the world's population; however, we generate 50% of all of the world's garbage (because of all of the stuff we buy).[5]

I am not saying you cannot buy nice stuff. You can spend your money whatever way you want, but maybe we should start savings some of our money as well. If anyone has the ability to save, it is us.

If saving is a good thing, why doesn't everyone save? Some of the answers I receive range from, "I have too many bills and debt," to "I don't make enough," to "I don't know how to save nor invest." There is a proverb that says, "The wise have wealth and luxury, but fools spend whatever they get."[6] This proverb is saying that it is foolish to spend everything you make.

By default people will tend to spend everything they make. To save you must make a conscience effort to do so. Saving and building wealth is not easy. If it were easy everyone would save. Since 76% of Americans live paycheck to paycheck, most households are barely making it to the next paycheck, and they are not saving any of their income.[7] But you can be different. You can be the weird person in your community that actually keeps some of their hard earned money.

Sometimes when speaking to certain groups some people will be nervous about saving money. They see money as a bad thing that should not be held onto. I think this comes from the misquoted Bible verse, "Money is the root of all evil." This is not what it says. The actual verse is in 1 Timothy 6:10, which says, "For the **love** of money is a root of all kinds of evil." (emphasis added). Notice that it is the love of money that causes people to do all kinds of evil acts. It is not money itself that causes evil.

Money is not good nor evil. It is simply a tool or instrument. I like to think of money like a brick. You can take a stack of bricks and make something great like a home, or a football stadium. You can also take a brick and throw it through a window and cause damage to someone's property. The brick is amoral. It does not have morals. It simply does whatever the owner uses it for. The same is true with money.

Money can be used for good such as helping the homeless get a meal or to purchase clothes for those that are in need. That same money could also be used to buy weapons that could be used to harm someone. The money itself is not good nor bad.

Therefore, saving money for your family's future is a good idea. Once you are able to save some money, you can begin to earn more money with your saved money. In other words, your money begins to work for you. And if you get enough money working, then you do not need to work. You get to retire.

Saving for College

If you have kids, one of the areas that you have probably thought about savings for is college. As a college professor I see firsthand how much students pay for their college tuition, books, fees, room, and board. It is not cheap, which is why some parents try to save money to help out their children during their college years.

529 Plan

The government understands the benefit of having parents save money for their children's college, so they have created laws that provide tax benefits for doing so. The 529 plan is one way to save for college and save in taxes.

A 529 plan allows you to put money into an account that can be used for tuition, books, fees, computer technology, room, and board.[8] You can put in as much as your child will need for their college costs. The benefit of this type of account is that any income you make is not taxable. So if you begin saving early and your investment increases substantially, you are able to use all of the money without having some of it go to pay taxes.

These plans are vary from state to state, so it is important that you research the rules for your particular state. These plans can be set up for anyone (the person does not have to be your child). You can establish a plan for a relative, a friend, or even yourself.

Educational Savings Account

Another way to save money for college is through an Educational Savings Account (ESA) or sometimes called an Education IRA. ESAs are similar to 529 plans in that you put money into an account for college. ESAs allow money to be used for qualified elementary and secondary education costs. However, there is an annual limit for ESAs. At the time of the writing of this book you can contribute up to $2,000 per child per year into an ESA account.[9] So if you put $2,000 per year into an account from the time your child is born until they are 18 years old, you will have saved $36,000. If that money is invested in the account and earns a 12% rate of return, the account will grow to $111,500 by the time the child is 18 years old. That means you will have earned a profit of $75,500, which is tax free, and can be used for educational expenses for your child. This benefit make ESA accounts an attractive investment tool for education.

ESAs also differ from 529 plans in that the ESA money must be used on a person that is 30 years old or younger. Also the amount that can be saved each year may be reduced for people that have high levels of income. Overall the 529 plan and ESA are great ways to save for college while receive a tax incentive at the same time.

Saving is a great way to build your family's defense. Remember that offense wins games, but defense wins championships. So let's find ways to strengthen our defense through saving.

Questions for Study

1. What are some reasons to save money?
2. Why doesn't everyone save money?
3. Can everyone save money?
4. When is the best time to start saving? If you could go back in time, would you have started saving earlier in life?

7

PLAYING SMARTER NOT HARDER

In 2004 the US Men's Basketball team was competing for the gold medal in the summer Olympics in Athens. The championship game was between the United States and the Puerto Rico National Basketball Team. The US team was composed of all-star players from the NBA. This Olympic team included many of the best players in the world.

In the final game Puerto Rico beat the United States and won the gold medal. This was the first time the US had ever lost a basketball game in the Olympics since NBA players were allowed to compete.

In basketball, as well as in many sports, it is not always about having the most talent. Some teams are able to win because they are smarter. The same is true with investing. Investing smarter will outperform any other investment strategy. To invest smarter you need to know a little about investing.

So, are you ready to do some investing? Are you thinking about playing the stock market, but you don't know where to start? Well, you have come to the right place. Let's begin by talking about the game of roulette.

Roulette is a very popular game that is played in Las Vegas. (Now I do not advocate gambling, but this game will illustrate my point). In roulette a ball is spun around a wheel that contains 38 numbers. The easiest bet is black or red. Since about half the numbers are black and about half are red, if you bet $100 on black, and the ball lands on a black number, you double your money. This is the lowest risk bet you can make. Since it is a low risk bet, the payout is also very low. On the other hand if you bet on one number, let's say seven, and the ball lands on seven, you win 36 times your bet. So, the one hundred dollar bet would pay out $3,600! The reason the payout is so high is because there is a high risk that you will lose, so they compensate by offering a high reward if you win.

Now you might be wondering, "What does this have to do with investing?" The answer is everything. Just like in roulette low risk equals low reward, and high risk equals high reward. The same is true in investing. The more you risk in the type of investment you make, the more "potential" reward you could make.

Let's think of investing risk as a spectrum. On one end you have little to no risk. And on the other side you have very high risk, and there is a range of risk in between. Your first task is to determine how much risk you are willing to take. Some people don't like uncertainty, and want very little risk. Others are willing to take a shot with the hopes of getting a big payout.

The amount of risk you take in investing will depend on many things. Typically the more time you have until you have to invest the more risk you will take. So, a young person that is just beginning their career might go with some high risk growth stocks, and someone who is close to retirement might focus on some conservative bonds.

Wherever you are on the risk spectrum, it is probably a good idea to diversify. Just like in baseball it is better to have nine good players than to just have one great player. In other words don't put all your investments in one high risk investment. If the economy goes south, you will lose much of your investment if you are not diversified. If you do want high risk stocks, you can invest heavily in those types of investments; however, you still want to invest in some other categories, even if it is a smaller percentage.

Ok, so what are low risk investments, and what are high risk investments? Well, the safest you can do with your money is to do nothing. In other words, don't invest it at all. There is no risk, but there is also no return. You are guaranteed to have the same amount of money that you started with. People do need money to pay monthly bills, so everyone has some cash in a checking account or cash in their wallet that is not being invested.

Government Securities

Next to doing nothing, one of the safest investments is investing is government securities. A government security simply means that you are letting the government borrow some of your money. In return, they will pay you back with interest. There are few different options when it comes to government securities such as Treasury bonds, Treasury bills, and Treasury notes. These investments are considered low risk because the US government always pays back its debt. Some people even consider these investments close to zero risk because the government can pay you back no matter what (remember they own the printing presses and can make more money if they run out). As we learned earlier, low risk means low reward. And that is true with government securities. They pay some of the lowest rates out of any investment you can make. As an example, the one year Treasury Bill rate on February 3, 2025 was 4.2%.[1] That is less than one percent. That means it would take about 16.85 years to double your money.[2] That is a long time. Investing in government securities is like bunting the baseball. It is easier to hit the ball, but the ball isn't going to go very far.

Bank Savings

Most people do not want to invest all of their money in government securities because the interest is just too low. So what about saving your money at the bank? Banks are very low risk investments because a bank account is FDIC insured. That means that if the bank were to fail, the government would step in and guarantee that your money would still be there. In other words, investing at a bank is very low risk; therefore, the return is going to be very low.

As of the time of the writing of this book the interest rate on savings accounts is .01-5%. One of the bigger banks in America that I just looked up is paying .01% per year. That means if you save one hundred dollars for a whole year at the bank, they will pay you one penny in interest at the end of the year. You aren't going to be able to build wealth at that rate.

Now even though savings accounts pay next to nothing in interest, that does not mean you should not have them. Everyone needs at least one savings account. These accounts can be used for many things. For example, you will want one savings account for your emergency fund. The benefit of savings accounts is that you can have quick access to the money if needed. In technical terms the money is liquid. When emergencies happen you don't have time to sell a piece of real estate in order to use the money, so you use savings accounts for your emergency fund. You can also use savings accounts for other short term saving. Remember savings accounts are free. You can have as many as you want. I have at least a dozen. You can make one for each of your kids to teach them how to save. You can have one for a vacation you are setting money aside for. You can have one for a car you want to save for. You can have one for a down payment on a home you want to save for. It is completely up to you. By having an account it is easier to keep your money separated by what you want to use it for. Now remember that the interest rate will be very low, so I only use savings accounts as a way to organize my money for the short term.

Certificate of Deposit

For most people a savings account pays too low of an interest rate. So banks offer another instrument called a CD, or certificate of deposit. A CD is basically a savings account where your money is locked up for a specific amount of time. This allows the bank to use your money for lending purposes, which allows them to pay you a higher interest rate. The interest rate you get depends on how long you are willing to invest your money at the bank, and the amount you are willing to invest. The current interest rate on a CD is 1-5% if you give the bank your money for one year to five years. This is not much higher than the savings account we discussed above, which is why many people have stopped investing in CDs as a viable investment.

Savings and CD interest rates haven't always been this low. In the 1980s interest rates were much higher. You could invest in a CD and earn over 10% each year![3] That is a far cry from less than 1% today at some banks. So, because of the low interest rates (which are controlled by the Federal Open Market Committee), interest rates continue to be extremely low. This is good when you want to borrow money because you get a low interest rate, but it isn't good when you want to save money.

Corporate Bonds

So if banks are paying low rates of return, where can you go to get a higher rate. The answer is corporate bonds. Corporate bonds are like a base hits in baseball. They aren't fancy, but they eventually scores runs. A bond is simply a fancy word for a loan. Some companies want to borrow money, but they don't want to go to a bank. Instead, they want to borrow the money from the public, so they can issue a bond. So think of a bond as loaning a company money so that they can run their business. For example, let's say a university wants to build a new stadium on campus. The cost is going to be $100 million. The school does not have that much money in their savings, so they decide to issue bonds to the public so that they can begin building the stadium. You and I buy the bonds, and over time we are paid interest, and eventually will be repaid our principal.

Bonds are given grades just like we receive when in school. The grades are A, B, C, and D. Really good, safe bonds are given an A. These are very low risk bonds issued by big companies that can easily pay back the bond. B bonds are higher risk but are still considered a good investment. C bonds are even higher risk, and D bonds are very high risk and are sometimes called junk bonds.

Remember that there is a tradeoff between risk and reward. Therefore, A bonds have low risk which means they will pay a low rate of interest. D bonds are high risk, so they must pay higher rates of interest to motivate people to invest in them. Most investors stick with A or B bonds. These are considered investment grade. C and D bonds are getting closer to gambling than investing, so major investment companies stay away from these. A and B bonds are a very popular investment that people use as part of their investment strategy.

There are a couple organizations that grade bonds, and their grading systems are slightly different (one uses AAA, AA, and A) to grade really good A bonds versus lower quality A bonds.

So how do bonds work? Remember, a bond is basically a loan. Most bonds sell for around $1,000. So you could spend $5,000 and buy five bonds. Once you purchase the bond, you will begin earning interest and will receive a payment once or twice a year. You will continue to receive interest payment until the bonds mature, then you will get your principal back. Bonds can last for up to 30 years. The company will tell you how long the bond is good for. So if you purchase a five year bond for $1,000, then you will receive interest payments for five years and then get $1,000 at the end of five years. When you purchase a five year bond, that does not mean you need to keep it for five years. You can sell it at any time. Whoever buys the bond from you will get the remaining interest that is earned.

There are two ways to make money on bonds. One is the interest rate (or coupon rate) of the bond. This is the interest you receive each year for owning the bond. The second way to earn money is from the discount on the bond. Remember most bonds sell for about $1,000. So if you buy a bond for $900, when the bond is mature, it will be worth $1,000. So you will make an extra $100 at the end of the bond's life. This is called a discount bond. You are getting the bond at a discount (less than $1,000). Some bonds are sold at a premium (more than $1,000) Why would someone pay more than $1,000 for a bond that is only going to be worth $1,000 in the future? The answer is the coupon rate is really high, so people are willing to pay more up front for the higher interest rate they will receive over time. In summary bonds can sell at a discount (less than one thousand) or at a premium (over one thousand).

So what kind of interest rate do bonds pay? Remember it depends on the risk or grade of the bond. As of the time of this book the rate of 20 year A bonds is 4.89%.[4] The B bonds will pay a higher rate, and the C bonds even higher.

Municipal Bonds

Bonds that are issued by states, cities, and countries to build schools, highways and other large projects are called municipal bonds. These bonds are attractive to investors because the interest that is earned is tax free. So you can save between 10-40% depending on the tax bracket you are in and how long you keep the bonds. Since municipal bonds offer a tax break, they do pay a lower rate of interest than other corporate bonds.

Stocks

So a bond is a loan to a company. Then what is stock? Stock is ownership in a company. So if you go and buy one share of McDonald's stock, does that mean you are part owner of McDonald's? The answer is yes. Does that mean you can walk into the restaurant and get free Big Macs? The answer is no. So what does owning stock entitle you to? Owning stock entitles you to a share of the company's profits. So if McDonald's sells lots of Big Macs, you make money. If they don't sell a lot of Big Macs because everyone is now going to Chick-fil-A, then you lose money. So stocks are higher risk. Think of investing in stocks as swinging for the homerun. Sometimes you will hit a homerun, and sometimes you will strike out. In other words, there is no guarantee that you will make money. Since you are taking on more risk, companies have to compensate you for that by paying a higher reward. The stock market on average has earned about 10% per year. Some stock make more, and some make less. This is a much higher rate of return than savings accounts and bonds, but it also has much higher risk.

There are two ways to make money on stocks. The first way is through dividends. A dividend is simply when a company decides to give money to all of the owners. So they might decide to pay a $.25 dividend. That means that for every share of stock you own you will get $.25. So if you own 1,000 share you will get $250 (1,000 x $.25). Companies that pay dividends usually pay every quarter (every three months). Some people like to buy stocks and then live on the dividend income that is generated.

Companies do not have to pay dividends. Some companies never pay dividends. So then how do people make money if they do not receive dividends? The answer is capital gains. Capital gains is a fancy way of saying buy low and sell high. So the second way to make money is to sell your stock for more than you paid. Remember that there is no guarantee that the stock will go up in value, so there is some risk involved. But if the company is successful, the stock price should go up, and you should be able to generate a profit.

Mutual Funds

Have you ever been looking at the appetizers while at a restaurant and just can't make up your mind? You want to try them all, but you don't want to have to buy 10 appetizers. Then you get excited when you see the appetizer called the "sampler platter". On the sampler platter you get a few shrimp, a few potato skins, a few chicken wings, (anyone getting hungry), a little bit of this, and a little bit of that. A mutual fund is very similar to the sampler platter. Instead of just buying one stock, you can buy one mutual fund that contains lots of stocks. For example if you want to invest in international companies, you can purchase an international mutual fund (which only has international stocks). This way you do not have to go out and buy stock in each of these international companies. Or if you want to invest in only small startup companies, then you can purchase a mutual fund with small startup stocks. Want to invest in only large companies? No problem. Only technology companies? No problem. There are literally thousands of mutual funds to choose from.

One of the benefits of a mutual fund is diversification. Diversification is a fancy way of saying don't put all of your eggs in one basket. For example, if I went out and bought Google stock, and then the company went bankrupt, I would lose all of the money that I invested. However, if I purchased a technology based mutual fund that invested in one hundred technology companies, then all one hundred companies would have to go bankrupt for me to lose all of my money. So being diversified is a very important part of investing. And mutual funds allow you to diversify without spending too much money.

Mutual funds are probably the most popular investment. They are so popular that some people only invest in mutual funds. Mutual funds have averaged about 9% rate of return over the last several decades. This is a slightly lower rate than stock (10%), but that is because you are taking on less risk when you invest in mutual funds than investing in just one company's stock. Mutual funds are also the typical investment for 401K plans and pension plans.

In order to purchase a mutual fund you will need a brokerage account. Most of the large banks offer a brokerage account, or you can go to a brokerage firm (such as Charles Schwab). There are also online brokerage firms that offer inexpensive ways to purchase stocks, bonds, and mutual funds. Companies like E*TRADE is a popular online brokerage firm.

Once you select a company, you can open an account and make a deposit. Then you can connect your checking account to your brokerage account so that you can make transfers as needed into or out of your account. After you have some money in your account, you can purchase any stock, bond, or mutual fund you want. It is just that easy.

Before you buy or invest anything it is always good to do some research before you invest. Some people invest simply because they use a company's product. For example, someone might want to buy Starbucks stock because they drink their coffee every day. That might sound like a good idea, but what if the company is actually losing money. It is wise to research before making a decision.

If you prefer to have someone invest your money for you, brokerage firms do offer that service for a fee. In summary everyone should have a brokerage account so that they can begin saving and investing.

When is the best time to start saving and investing? A wise man once said that the best time to plant a tree is 20 years ago, and the second best time is right now. The same is true in our finances. The best time to begin saving was 20 years ago, or in your 20s. Most of us did not start then, so the second best time is right now. Don't wait another year to begin saving and investing. Get started now. Even if it is a small amount. Save something lest you save nothing.

Real Estate

Stocks, bonds, and mutual funds are good investments, but other people prefer to invest in something more tangible. Real estate is a popular investment because it involves physical property instead of something intangible like stock.

Investing in real estate can take on many forms. Some people might purchase a piece of land for investment purposes. They will hold onto the land with the hopes of one day reselling the land for a higher price.

Other people purchase property for the purpose of renting it in order to generate rental income. Rental property can include a rental home, an apartment complex, or a commercial shopping center.

Investments in real estate generally require a larger investment than purchasing stock, so not everyone is able to invest in real estate. Real estate also has risk because there is the risk that the property declines in value, or that the property does not generate enough rental income to cover the costs involved. Therefore, before purchasing any rental property you should calculate all of the expenses and the projected revenue to see if you will have a positive cash flow. Robert Kiyosaki, author of the book *Rich Dad Poor Dad* believes you should always have a positive cash flow when dealing with rental properties. Investors should not purchase rental property knowing that they will be losing money each month because hopefully one day the property will increase in value. The property should generate a profit from the beginning, or it is not worth investing in.

In summary, investing in real estate does involve some risk; however, if the risk pays off there can be substantial rewards. Some people have made millions on real estate, and others have lost money. It is important to do your homework and research before making any large investment decision.

Hard Assets

A hard asset is an investment that you can actually hold (such as gold, silver, platinum, etc.). Hard assets typically go in the opposite direction of the stock market. So when the stock market is going down, the value of gold and silver goes up. (That is why people invest in gold in silver when they anticipate that the economy is going to decline in the future).

The easiest way to invest in gold and silver is to purchase a gold or silver eagle coin. These coins are issued from the US Treasury, and they contain 99.99% pure gold or silver. There are many companies and countries selling coins; however, the eagles are the most popular because they are issued by the US government.[5]

An eagle is one ounce of metal. So, a gold eagle is one ounce of gold. Investors can also purchase less than an ounce of metal. For example, there are half eagles (a half ounce), and tenth eagles (one-tenth of an ounce).

These coins increase in value two ways. One is based on the value of gold and silver. As these metals increase in value so does the value of the coin. In addition, some investors collect the coins by year, so the older the coin, the more value it will sell for. Investment advisors typically recommend that investors should have about 10% of their investment in hard assets.

Futures and Options

So far we have covered many different types of

investments from low risk (government securities) to high risk (stocks and real estate). There are investments that have even higher risk than stocks, and they are called future and options. These investments are basically betting on the future price of something. For example, you can purchase a future's contract on the price of a barrel of oil one year from now. If the price of oil goes above the price of the future's contract, you make money. If the price ends up below the contract price, then your investment is worth nothing.

Futures and options are very high risk investments if you do not own the underlying commodity, and in my opinion, should not be used as an investment strategy for the average investor.

Gambling

Of course, if you want to go even higher on the risk scale, you can resort to all out gambling. I do not recommend this as your investment strategy, but there are many people spending money trying to win it big by gambling.

I also would not recommend gambling as a means to increase how much money you have. I lived in Las Vegas for four years while going to college, and at one time I worked as an accountant for one of the large casinos. Remember, they do not build billion dollar casinos because people normally win money. People lose money, and they lose lots of it. In fact, the longer you play, the more you lose. As the accountant, I knew how much people would lose on average every hour they played. The slot machines made so much per hour, the table games made so much per hour, etc. There is a phrase, "The house always wins." And it is true. The casino comes out a winner every week, while the people gambling keep losing.

You may not live in a city where gambling is legal, but most states have a lottery that people can play. The lottery is not an investment strategy you should pursue. Dave Ramsey likes to say that the lottery is a tax on people that can't do math. It is true. The odds of winning the lottery are so low that you have a much better chance of getting in an accident driving your car to purchase the ticket than you ever have of actually winning.

In 2022 Americans spent over $97 billion on lottery tickets.[6] That is more than Americans spent on video games, books, music, and sporting events. People really think they have a shot at winning. People that make under $10,000 a year that play the lottery spend $597 a year on lottery tickets.[7] If that same person invested that $597 from age 20 to 65 in a mutual fund, they would have a three quarters of a million dollars when they retired. That is a much better investment than wasting money on lottery tickets.

Even those people that do win the lottery often say that

having that much money is not necessarily a good thing. There have been many lottery winners that have regretted winning the lottery because of what it did to their family. The problem is that people think all of their problems will go away if they had millions of dollars. This is simply not true.

Evelyn Adams won the $5.4 million dollar New Jersey lottery in 1985. Then she won it a second time in 1986. You would think she would be happy and enjoy her winnings. Instead she gambled most of it away and is broke today.

In 2002, Jack Whittaker won $314.9 million in Powerball lottery. At the time it was the largest individual payout in U.S. lottery history. After winning the lottery, he encountered numerous tragedies with the new found money, from a divorce to even the death of his granddaughter from a drug overdose. Jewell Whittaker, Jack's ex-wife had this to say about the lottery, "If I knew what was going to transpire, honestly, I would have torn the ticket up."

The stories go on and on of people who did not find happiness from winning the lottery. In fact, the number of people that have found themselves worse off after winning the lottery has led to the phrase "lottery curse" to be used for all of these people. Money did not solve these people's problems. You may be thinking, "Well I know that money doesn't solve ALL problems, but it does solve some problems (such as not having enough money to pay the bills)." However winning the lottery doesn't even solve lottery winners money problems. Nearly one third of multimillion dollar lottery winners become bankrupt in just a few short years after their big win.

So to summarize, investing in bonds and mutual funds is a great way to invest for most people. Gambling is not a good strategy. By consistently hitting base hits and doubles through investing, you will score runs, and those runs will lead to wins.

Questions for Study

1. Is investing only for wealthy people?

2. What are the different types of investments that you can invest in?

3. What is the benefit of investing in a risky investment? What is the benefit of investing in a low risk investment?

4. Do you see yourself as a low risk, medium risk, or high risk investor? Does the amount of risk you are willing to accept change over your life?

8

BUYING THE STADIUM

Imagine that you are a high school football coach, and each year for the past five years your team has won the state championship. Are you ready to buy the ultimate stadium so that you team can feel like they are really successful? WAIT. Before you jump into this colossal project it might be a good idea to see if you can afford it. I know that may not be popular to hear, but why spend $100 million on the new high school stadium for your team, when the football program only generates $3 million a year in ticket sales?

For most people their stadium, i.e. their home, is their largest expense. And since it is their largest expense it is the one item that can easily influence a family's overall financial situation. Most people buy a home they cannot afford. They are what we call "house poor." They have a nice big house, yet they can't afford other necessities in life, and they don't have any money left over to save.

So how much is too much when buying a stadium or home? Some real estate people say that you shouldn't spend more than 2.5 times your annual salary on your home. So, if your family makes $100,000, then you can spend 2.5 times that, or a maximum of $250,000 on a home. Personally I prefer to stay closer to 2 times the family income or a $200,000 home in this example. Either way, this is a quick and easy way to figure out how much a family can afford on home.

Another way to figure out how much to spend on a home is based on a percentage of your take home pay. The goal is to spend no more than one third of your money on your rent or mortgage payment. So, if your family earns $7,000 per month (after taxes and deductions) then you can spend no more than $2,333 per month on your home.

If you add all of your utilities, HOA fees, and maintenance with the mortgage payment (or rent), the total should not be more than half of your income.

At this point some of you are calculating your how much you can afford based on your income, and you are feeling discouraged. Please do not feel that way. Having a big home is NOT going to make you happy. Keeping up with the Jones is NOT going to make you happy. Keeping up with the culture or your desires is NOT going to make you happy. Living within your means will bring you so much more peace than overspending ever will. I have lived in apartments, and I have lived in houses. I wasn't any less happy when I lived in an apartment than when I lived in a house. My happiness was not based on the size of my home. Of course, it would be nice to have a bigger and better place to live. But I must be able to afford wherever I decide to live.

The biggest mistake I see people make is that they spend too much on a new home because they just got married or just had their first baby. They feel like they need a new home to go with their new stage in life. The problem is that they did not sit down and calculate what they could really afford, and they end up overspending on their home. Why add unnecessary stress to a new family? Overbuying on a home WILL lead to financial stress and arguments over money and can eventually causes some couples to divorce. It is not worth it. Live within your means, and when your income increases, then you can get the bigger home.

Home Financing

Once you've figured out how much of a stadium (home) you can afford, you are ready to go to the bank to see about a loan. You will see several different types of loans and interest rates, and some of it can be confusing. The length of a home loan can vary. Most loans are for 30 years. However, you can get 20 year, 15 year, and 10 year loans also. Most people will focus on the 30 year loans.

Back when I played football the coaches always posted that I weighed more than I really did. They did this to make the team look bigger than it really was. So there was my advertised size, and my actual size. The same is true with home loans. When comparing loans there are two rates you will see. There is the interest rate and annual percentage rate (APR).

You always want to focus on the APR and compare loans based on this number. The APR is the true interest rate with compounding factored into the loan. Banks are required to disclose this number because this is the true cost of getting the loan. The interest rate has no value to me as a borrower. I am only concerned about the APR. The reason I mention this is that sometimes banks will advertise the interest rate (and not focus on the APR) because the interest rate is always lower than the APR. Don't fall for this marketing ploy. Always ask for the APR.

Points

There are also points associated with some loans. Think of points like a signing bonus when hiring a professional player. In other words points are a fancy way of saying, "prepaid interest." For example, if a loan has 2 points, that means that you are prepaying 2% of the loan value in interest in exchange for a lower rate. So if I wanted to get a loan for $100,000, and there are 2 points on the loan, then I would have to pay $2,000 ($100,000 x 2%) in interest up front in order to get the loan. Banks offer points in order to give you a lower interest rate on your loan. The more points you pay, the lower the interest rate. In other words, the more money you give them now, the less they will charge you later.

The real question is, "Should I pay for points to get a lower interest rate?" The answer depends on how long you plan on living in the home. If you think you will live in the home for the full 30 years, then the answer is easy. Get the points. However most people do not stay in their home that long. The average homeowner stays in a home about 7 years. So if you do not see yourself staying in your home for a long period of time, it may not benefit you to pay for points. In other words, why would you want to give the bank so much money up front to get a lower rate when you aren't going to stay there that long to enjoy the lower rate?

Whether you end up buying points or not, you should begin by comparing loans based on the interest rate with zero points. This is the true interest rate. The banks like to advertise loan with the points because it makes them SEEM more affordable. But remember if you are buying points you need to pay that money upfront. Three points on a $200,000 home is $6,000. The bank will want $6,000 from you plus the regular closing costs when you sign for the loan. If you don't have that much money saved, then forget about points, because points basically increase the required down payment.

Adjustable Rate Mortgages

Ok, enough about points. Now let's discuss the type of loan you will get. There are fixed mortgages and adjustable rate mortgages (ARMs). Fixed loans are fairly obvious. The rate never changes, it remains fixed. So if the interest rate is 4% when the loan is issued, it remain at 4% for the life of the loan. An ARM loan, however, will remain fixed for a certain period of time, and then it will vary based on the current interest rate. The fixed time period could be three years, five years, seven years, etc. What makes these loans attractive is that the fixed rate will be lower than the loans that are fixed for the entire period of the loan. So when people are comparing loans, they might see a 4% fixed loan, and a five year ARM that is 3.5%. On the surface it might seem that the ARM is cheaper, but remember that after five years, the ARM interest rate will change, and the interest rate may go up and up and up based on the current interest rate.

One thing to consider when getting an ARM is how long you plan on living in the home. If you know you probably won't stay in the home longer than seven years, then maybe the seven year ARM would fit your needs, because you will be moving before the adjustable rate kicks in.

Think of the difference between fixed rate and ARM like the difference between a player with a contract versus the free agent. The player with the contract has a salary that is locked in, just like a fixed mortgage. However the free agent's salary changes each year depending on how they perform, just like the ARM changes based on the market rate.

Refinancing

Some of you have owned a home for some time now, and you have been getting mail that it is time to refinance. Should you do this? Refinancing means that you are going to pay off your current loan by getting a new loan. The goal would be that the interest rate on the new loan is lower than the rate on the old loan, which would save you money.

The first thing to consider is how much lower is the new rate compared to the old rate. Most people recommend that the new rate must be more than 1% less than the current rate you are paying on your loan for it to be worth refinancing. Remember that when you refinance you are basically getting a new loan. So the bank is going to charge you closing costs just like when you bought the home. Therefore, if your new interest rate is not at least 1% less than the current rate, you will lose money because the closing costs will be greater than the interest saved.

If you can save more than 1% on the rate of your loan, you are ready for step two. The next step is deciding how long you want to refinance the new loan for. This is very important. You have a couple options. First, you can get a new loan that somewhat matches the years you have remaining on your current loan. For example, if you have 19 years left on your loan, you can get a 20 year mortgage when you refinance. Most banks advertise mortgages in increments of five years. So there are 30 year, 25 year, 20 year, 15 year, etc. loans. Some banks will also give you a loan for however many years you want (between 1 and 30 years).

The second option is to refinance and get a 30 year loan. This is a VERY tempting option. The reason it is so tempting is because your monthly loan payment will go down significantly. That is very appealing to most people. So what is the catch? The catch is that you are starting all over on your loan. Instead of having let's say 19 years left on your mortgage you now have 30 years left. You are starting all over.

If you would like to have your home paid off one day, I would not recommend the 30 year option when refinancing. I would recommend that you get a loan that closely matches the number of years you have left on your current loan.

Home Equity Loans

The other temptation when refinancing is to pull out equity from your home. Let's say that you have been paying on your home for 10 years and owe $100,000, and the home is now worth $175,000. Some people will refinance their home for $150,000, so that they can get $50,000 in cash from the bank with their new loan. I know this sounds tempting, but what is the catch. The catch is that this is a loan, which means you will need to pay back the $50,000. In other words, your mortgage payment will go up because you are now borrowing more money. I generally do not recommend this option. This will just get you further into debt.

Now some people have reasoned that they will refinance and get some cash back so that they can pay off some other debts that they have. For instance they decide to pull out $20,000 in equity so that they can pay off the credit cards and some other outstanding debts they have. They reason that the interest rate on their home is lower than what they are paying on their credit cards, so they will be saving money each month on interest.

There are a couple problems with this logic. First by

paying off the credit card debt with refinanced money you are basically taking unsecured debt and making it into secured debt. Secured debt means that if you do not make a payment, the bank can take something from you. For example, mortgages are secured by the house that is associated with the loan. So if you do not pay your mortgage payment, the bank has the right to take your house. Car loans are the same way. Credit card debt, however, is unsecured. This means that there is nothing the bank can take from you if you decided not to pay your credit card. The most the bank can do is charge you interest and fees and send your debt to collections.

So if you take your refinanced money and pay off the credit cards, you have basically said that if I do not pay my credit card debt you can now take my home. That is why you need to carefully consider whether you should use refinanced money to pay off credit card debt.

The other thing to consider is how you got into credit card debt in the first place. If you pay off your credit cards using your refinanced money, who's to say that you won't charge up your credit cards again? If you don't make any changes in your spending habits you may find yourself back in credit card debt in addition to the credit card debt that is now attached to your house.

Paying Off The Home

For many people the goal is to one day have the house paid off. That is a great goal, and it is very achievable if you plan ahead. One way to pay off the house is to simply pay the loan payment each month for 30 years. Over time the loan balance will go down to zero. I recommend that families compare the number of years left on the loan to their retirement age. If you can get these numbers to closely match you will be in good shape. In other words if you can have the house paid off by the time you retire, this will be a tremendous help to your budget during those years of your life.

Another option is to pay extra money each month to decrease the number of years that you have to pay on your home. One strategy is to make one extra loan payment a year. To do this easily some people make a loan payment once every four weeks instead of once a month. Since there are 52 weeks in a year, by making a loan payment once every four weeks you will end up making 13 payments throughout the year.

Another strategy would be to pay an extra one twelfth of the loan payment each month. So if your loan payment is $1,200 each month you would simply pay an extra $100 ($1,200/12) each month. At the end of the year you would have made an extra payment each year. So what is the benefit of paying an extra loan payment each year? If you had a

$200,000 home, your interest rate was 4%, and you made an extra payment each year, you would pay off your home 50 months faster! That would equate to saving $23,000 in interest! No bad for simply paying one extra payment per year.

Whatever strategy you and your family decide to implement, paying off your home is a great goal, and one that will benefit you for the rest of your life.

Some people wonder if they should use their savings to pay off their home. Maybe they are getting closer to retirement age, and they have accumulated enough in their savings to pay off the remaining balance on their home. On the one hand, they can pay off their home and have no mortgage payment, which would save interest and give them peace of mind that their home is paid off. On the other hand, they could keep their savings, which they might need when they retire, and they would continue to have the tax deduction from the mortgage interest.

The answer to this question depends on your situation. For most people the tax deduction does not justify having a mortgage. For example, if you are the 25% tax bracket and you spend $8,000 in interest for the year, you will end up saving only $2,000 in taxes. So it would be better to save $8,000 by not having a mortgage than to save $2,000 by having a mortgage and tax break. So most people should not keep a mortgage just because they get a tax break.

However if your savings is generating a good return, it might make sense to keep the mortgage. For example, if the money you are investing is making 8%, and your mortgage is 3%, then you are making 5% after paying the interest on your mortgage (and you still get the tax break on the interest). In this case, financially it would be better to keep the mortgage.

As you can see the decision really depends on your individual situation. There are a few additional situations you should avoid. It is generally not a good idea to use money that you were planning to put into a 401K if it means that you will miss out on the employer matching program. Remember you always want to put into your 401K at least what your employer is willing to match. This is free money that you do not want to miss out on. So it is normally in your best interest to invest in your 401K at least what your employer will match, instead of using the money to pay down the mortgage if the choice is between these two options.

Also some people are faced with the question of pulling money out of their 401K early to pay off the mortgage. Again this is generally not a good idea. When you take money out of a 401K early you are generally subject to a penalty of 10%, and you have to pay taxes on the money withdrawn. This strategy is not recommended. As you can see there are many factors to consider when paying off your home. Generally it is a good goal to have no mortgage payment by the time you retire;

however, you want to consider the factors we discussed before making that decision. About 75% of people who are retired have no mortgage payment.[1] This is a goal that you too can reach if it makes sense for your family.

Questions for Study

1. What are some things to consider when buying a home?

2. What are points, adjustable rate mortgages, and refinancing?

3. Should paying off your house before you retire be part of your retirement strategy?

9

PREPARING FOR PLAYOFFS

Imagine a football coach working long hours to win every game of the season. The team is undefeated, and the whole school is excited. The coach finds out that they are going to the playoffs, but he is completely unprepared. He hasn't let his players know the day of the game, he hasn't scheduled practices for the players, and he hasn't studied the team that they will be playing. How successful do you think this team will be in the playoffs?

Did you know that one out of three working Americans have little to no money saved for retirement.[1] In other words they are not prepared for the playoffs. Is saving for retirement a good thing? There is a proverb that says, "Good people leave an inheritance to their grandchildren, but the sinner's wealth passes to the godly."[2] So if saving for retirement is a good thing, why is it that some Americans are not planning for the future? Is it lack of money, lack of wisdom, or just lack of forethought?

Most people would probably say that they do not want to work after retirement age. They might enjoy a part time job just to get out of the house, but they do not want to have a heavy burden to work hard when they are past retirement age.

So how do you get started? The first thing you want to do is to invest using the help of the US government. The government wants people to save for retirement. They do not want Social Security to be your only source of income when you retire. So the government has wisely made laws where you receive tax benefits for saving for retirement. So that is your first tip. You always want to save for retirement using tax favored dollars. In other words the government will allow you to save money on taxes if you save for retirement. Think about that. The government is willing to not get paid as much so that you can save for retirement. Take advantage of that.

How Much is Enough?

Many people want to save for retirement, but they have no idea how much they need to save. They never know if what they are setting aside each paycheck will be enough when they get ready to retire. As a general rule the average household should save about 15% of their income towards retirement.

In baseball there are three things you need to be good at to be successful. You need to be able to hit, catch, and throw. For retirement there are three basic ways to plan for retirement: Social Security, 401K, and IRAs.

Saving through Social Security is easy because it is mandatory. You are automatically paying 6.2% of your income to the federal government. Your employer is also paying 6.2% for a total of 12.4%. The way Social Security works is that the people who are working today are paying for the people that are retired today. The good news is that you will be able to collect money when you reach retirement age; the bad news is there is not an account with your name on it waiting for you to retire. It is almost like a legalized pyramid scheme. As long as people continue to work and pay into it, the pyramid will stay in tack.

Some people are starting to believe that there will not be any Social Security when they are ready to retire. That is not true. As long as people are working, there will be money for those who are retired. The government may need to raise the rate or decrease the benefits in the future to balance the budget, but there should be something for everyone who has paid into it.

The second strategy for retirement is the 401K. The name comes from the paragraph in the law that started this type of investment. This type of account allows employees to invest money in mutual funds with pre-tax dollars. That means you don't pay any taxes now (you wait until you withdraw the money). So you can have money from your paycheck put into a 401K account, and then you get to pick the type of investment you want to buy. The employer usually gives you about a dozen categories to choose from. For example, you may be able to invest in large companies or international companies or small start-up companies. You choose based on how much risk you want to take. The good news is you get to pick. The bad news is that you could lose money.

Most employers will match a certain amount of contributions that their employees make to the 401K account. You should always invest at least what the employer will match. For example, the employer may offer to match up to 3% of your pay. So, if you put in 3% of your paycheck your boss will also put in 3%. You have doubled your money instantly.

Employers offer matching as a benefit, but it also creates less job turnover because they usually require that you stay with the company a certain number of years to be vested (when you get to keep the matched portion).

After Social Security and 401K is the IRA. IRA stands for Individual Retirement Account. An IRA is similar to the 401K described above except you control it yourself. You open the account, you pick the investment, you buy and sell, and you make all of the decisions for the account. So the IRA gives you more choices, but it also requires more attention. As of 2025, individuals can contribute up to $7,000 per year into their IRA account. So a married couple could contribute up to $14,000 of their household income into their IRA accounts.

There are two types of IRA accounts. There is the traditional IRA and the Roth IRA. The difference between the two is when you pay the taxes. With a traditional IRA you pay no tax when you deposit the money, but you do pay tax when you retire and withdraw the money. The Roth IRA is the opposite. You make investments with money that is already taxed from your paycheck, and when you retire you do not have to pay any taxes on the money you put in, or on ANY OF THE PROFITS! This is a big benefit. Imagine if you put in $100,000 into your Roth IRA and when you retired it grew to $300,000. The profit that you made ($200,000) is not taxed, and will never be taxed. For this reason most people choose a Roth IRA over a traditional IRA.

Everyone should open up a Roth IRA TODAY. There is no cost to open an account, you can start the account with $5, and you can connect your checking account to your IRA and transfer money whenever you choose. There are a lot of companies that offer IRAs. E*TRADE and Charles Schwab are a couple examples if you do not know where to go.

Earlier I mentioned that families should work toward saving 15% of their income for retirement. So, as an example your savings could look like this: Social Security 6.2% (mandatory), 401K 3% (or other amount matched by employer), and IRA 5.8%, for a total of 15%. You could always save more than this, but this would be a good initial goal.

An additional type of investment for retirement is the home. Some people don't think of their home as a type of retirement plan, but it is. Since the home is typically the largest cost for most families, paying off a house would allow a family to live off of less income each month. That is why some families plan their mortgage to coincide with retirement. They make sure that the years left on their mortgage is less than their remaining working years. For example if a couple is fifty years old, and they plan on retiring at sixty five, then their mortgage should have no more than fifteen years on it.

As you can see, saving for retirement requires a multi-faceted approach. It is like a racecar. It takes multiple wheels on a racecar to support the weight of the person sitting in it. The same is true of retirement. There is the wheel of Social Security, the wheel of the 401K, the wheel of the IRA, and the wheel of a paid off home.

So you may be wondering, "How much will I actually have if I begin saving money for retirement?" The answer depends on the three factors: time, interest rate, and principal. If you increase any one of these three, you will have more when you retire. Time is pretty easy to understand. The more time you have to invest, the more you will have because interest and dividends accumulate over time. So the person that starts investing in their 20s will have more than the person in their 50s, even if they invest the exact same amount of money because the younger person is earning interest over a longer period of time.

The second factor is the interest rate. The higher the rate, the more you make. The average for the stock market is 10%. So if you can make 10% per year, you are doing great. The average for mutual funds is 9%, and the average for savings accounts is around 1-4%. So all things being equal, the higher the rate, the higher potential profit you can make.

The third factor is principal. The more you invest the more you will have at retirement. I have included a table for you to use to see how much you will need to save each month in order to have a half million dollars in your account when you retire.

For example if you are 55 years old and have 10 years to retire, you would need to save $3,100 a month to have a half million when you retire. On the other hand, if you are 20 years old, you only need to save $200 a month, because you have 45 years to save and invest.

Years to Retire	Interest	Monthly Savings	Value at Retirement Age
10	6%	$ 3,100	$500,000
20	6%	$ 1,100	$500,000
30	6%	$ 500	$500,000
40	6%	$ 255	$500,000
45	6%	$ 200	$500,000

This why it is important to begin saving today. Even if it is a small amount. Save something now so that you do not need to play catch up later in life.

So let's say you are able to save a half million when you retire. What does that mean when you turn 65? How much will you have to spend on a monthly basis? The answer depends on how long you expect to live after you retire. In the United States the average life expectancy of a man is 76 years. For women it is 81 years. So if the average man retires at 65 years old, and lives about another ten years then he could spend about $5,062 a month for the rest of his life.

On the other hand if you have a woman who is in good health and she lives twenty years past retirement age, she will have $3,030 per month for the rest of her life. And if you wanted to play it safe and ensure that you have money available for thirty years after you retire, then you can withdraw $2,387 per month before the retirement savings is exhausted. See the following table:

Years After Retiring	Interest	Retirement Savings	Monthly Withdraw
10	3%	$ 500,000	$ 5,062
20	3%	$ 500,000	$ 3,030
30	3%	$ 500,000	$ 2,387

Notice that the interest rate is listed at 3%. So these amounts are based on the idea that you would still be investing your retirement money and earning a 3% return up until the time the money is withdrawn.

And of course, if you had a million dollars saved at retirement, you could double each of the monthly withdraw amounts to calculate what your budget would be. Whatever your goal is, it would be a good idea to create a budget for the day that you retire. In other words, pretend that today is your retirement day. How much would you get from Social Security? How much could you withdraw each month from your 401K or pension? What bills would you still have? Figure out what your income and expenses will be, so that you can ensure that you are saving enough now for your retirement years.

Life Insurance

Part of planning for the future is planning for the unexpected. If you have a family or people who are depending on your income, then you should have life insurance. Life insurance is not one of those things we like to think about because we all believe we are going to live a long life. The reality is that long life is not promised to anyone. So it is important to have insurance to ensure that money will be available for your dependents if something were to happen to you.

Life insurance falls into two broad categories: term and whole. Term life insurance means that you have insurance for a period of time, and if you don't use it, then you don't get anything back. It is like having auto insurance. If you don't get in any accidents during the year, you don't get any money back.

Whole life insurance means that even if you don't die during the period of time covered by the policy you still can get some money back at the end. This type of policy is more expensive because you are getting some money back at the end.

There are also other variations of these two categories of insurance policies. Whichever type you decide to get is up to you, but everyone should have something. Insurance companies can help you decide which policy is best for you. Also some employers offer term insurance policies as a deduction from your paycheck.

It is recommended that you have three to ten times your annual salary in an insurance policy. If you had seven times your income in life insurance and something happened to you, your dependents could take the life insurance money and invest it at 7%, and the interest that is earned would be equivalent to your salary. In other words they could live the rest of their lives and would still receive in interest what you earned each year from working.

Three to ten times your salary may sound like a lot; however, insurance is cheaper than most people think. As I'm writing this book, the cost of a $500,000 life insurance policy for a healthy 35 year old man with a 20 year term policy is about $40 a month.[3]

Will

Planning for the future not only involves having life insurance, but it also includes having a will. When I speak to audiences, I am always amazed at how many people do not have a will. Even AARP did a study and found out that two out of five people over the age of 45 do not have a will.[4] Why is that? Is it because we don't like to think about our death? Is it something we put off because we believe we are going to live long lives? Or do we believe that wills are only for people that have large estates?

It doesn't matter who you are, you should have a will. Without a will the probate court will decide what to do with your stuff. I would much rather have a say, than to expect a judge to make a good decision about my belongings, and who will take care of my kids and pets. So you need to have a will.

I believe most people agree that it is a good idea to have a will, but they just don't know where to go to get one. The answer is simple. You can write your own will, you can get a template from the internet, or you can go to a lawyer and have them help you prepare one. The choice is yours. In addition I have included a template in the Appendix of this book that you can use for your will. Simply fill it out, get it notarized, and you have an official will. Writing a will is not an exact science, you can include what you want to include, and your will can be as simple as writing on the back of a napkin (although I don't recommend this).

So now that you know how to get started on your will, there are a few things you need to decide. First, you need to decide who your executor will be. The executor is the person who will do everything that is listed in your will. This person could be your spouse, an adult child, a friend, a relative, or a lawyer. The person you choose should be someone you trust. Remember, you will not be there to make sure everything is followed exactly. That is why you need someone that you can rely on, and that is good with managing money and administrative tasks. You probably don't want to put a cousin who has a gambling problem in charge of your estate. The executor will be in charge of paying your bills after you are gone, liquidating assets, and distributing them to the heirs.

Once you select an executor, you will want to ask that person if they are willing to carry out that duty when needed. You will also want to have one or two backup executors in case the person you selected is unable to perform the duties of the executor at the time of your death.

In your will you can be as specific or as general in terms of who gets what. Your will can be as general as saying everything goes to this one person, or half goes to one child and half to the other. You can also specify that certain items go to certain people. For example, you can list that a piece of jewelry goes to a specific family member, or that some money will be donated to a charity. It is completely up to you. When my wife's grandmother passed away, she had included in her will that a necklace be given to my wife. This meant so much to my wife because her grandmother had thought of her. You can do the same by designating some items to certain people. And they do not need to be items that have value. For example, you could leave something that has sentimental value to someone like a military veteran could leave their mementoes to a loved one. Or, someone's coin collection could be designated to another collector. It is up to you.

Once you have completed your will, you want to have a couple witnesses sign it, get it notarized, and then give a copy to your executor. That way they will know what to do if need be. You should keep the original in a place that is accessible if something were to happen to you. Some people keep their will in a safe in their home.

After you have finished your will, give a copy to the executor, and you are done. You can always make changes to the will if need be, but it is not required. People generally update their will after a significant life event. For example, a marriage, the birth of a child, adoption, a major purchase or inheritance, the death of a beneficiary or executor, and a divorce are all reasons why you may want to update your will. After you update your will you simply destroy the old one, so that you only have one will at a time.

Sometimes people ask if they can make one will for both them and their spouse. If you are married you will want to have two wills. One for you, and one for your spouse. Your wills may look almost identical (your will might leave everything to your spouse, and your spouse may leave everything to you). However, you still want to have two wills because it is very rare for two people to die at the same time. So the court needs to know what you want to do if only one of you passes away. Separate wills also help to deal with issues such as ex-spouses and children from a previous relationship. In addition, separate wills can address property that was obtained prior to the marriage.

Durable Power of Attorney

In addition to having a will, you may want to consider who you give durable power of attorney to. Durable power of attorney gives someone the legal right to handle your financial affairs should you become incapacitated or disabled. Without this, no one is able to access your bank accounts to pay your bills for you without a lengthy legal process.

Advance Directive

There are also power of attorney rights that can be assigned for medical purposes. A health care power of attorney, also called a "designation of health care surrogate", can be used to give a loved one the right to make your medical decisions for you if you are unable to make them yourself.

Estate Tax

When someone passes, their estate is given to their heirs. Depending on the size of their estate, the heirs may have to pay an inheritance or estate tax. The government does not like the idea of having a few families pass down millions or billions of dollars down from generation to generation. So that is why there is a tax. If you die and you leave your kids a home and a few thousand dollars, you don't have to worry about the estate tax. As of 2025 you only have to file an estate tax return if you have property that is worth more than $13.99 million dollars. Therefore, most people will not have to worry about the estate tax; however, those who know they will have to deal with it should get advice from a CPA or lawyer.

Living Trust

When someone dies the decisions for managing the estate is handled by probate. Probate is the court system that determines if you have a will and if the will is valid. If you do not have a will, then the state will follow the laws of the state to determine how to handle your property. Some people do not like to deal with the probate courts because all of the information is public, and it can be a slow process.

For those who want privacy and efficiency in handling their estate, there is a living trust. Think of a trust like creating a corporation. A corporation will continue to exist after the stockholders leave the company. The same is true with a trust. A trust will hold your assets, and when you die, they can be distributed to your beneficiary without having to deal with probate.

A revocable living trust is set up while you are alive. It is also revocable, which means you can cancel it at any time if you change your mind. I recommend you use a lawyer to help you set up your trust if that is what you decide to do. When creating a trust you will designate someone to be your trustee. This person will carry out your instructions for distributing property (similar to the executor of a will). Most people that establish a living trust will only put their large assets in the trust, and then they can still have a will for the other stuff. Overall a revocable living trust is a great way to transfer property to your heirs efficiently and maintain your financial privacy.

Last Words

In addition to having a will and designating someone to make your financial and medical decisions you may want to consider writing out your last words. Your last words is a document that you write that is one final message to your loved ones that are left behind. Some people have it read at their funeral as a way to comfort those that are grieving the loss of you. It is a great way to speak to those who are grieving after you are gone. Some people even include encouragement to their family that they are now in Heaven, and that they look forward to being reunited with them someday. Other people have recorded a video of themselves with encouraging or comforting words for their family and friends.

Preparing for the playoffs is something everyone should do. Let's save for retirement and have a will in place so we don't find ourselves like the coach that was unprepared for the playoffs.

Questions for Study

1. What are some different ways to be better prepared for retirement?

2. What is the difference between an IRA and a 401K? Should you invest in both?

3. Should you have a will if you are young and single? Why do people need a will?

10

THE ALL-STAR TEAM

Now that you have learned how to create a playbook for your finances, how to get debt free, and how to save for retirement, you might be thinking that the only thing left is to relax and turn on the cruise control. The problem with this way of thinking is that you will miss out on the greatest part of financial freedom: the All-Star Team. The point of this book is not for you to accumulate a big stack of money and then pass away. That would be pointless.

The real adventure is in giving. Using your finances to help others is the greatest thing you can do with your finances. Now you may be thinking that giving is counter to saving and investing. But that is because saving and investing is the means to giving. Think about it this way. You cannot participate in the ultimate goal of giving if you haven't saved any of your money. However, once you have developed the habit of living on less than you earn, it becomes easier to give. So the purpose of saving and investing is to allow you to freely give without hesitation.

Let's think about football for a minute. What if I thought the purpose of football practice every day was only so that I could get my body in shape? I would be missing the whole point of football practice. The point of football practice is so that I will do better during the football games, so that my team can win. Yes, my body will get in shape in the process, but that is not my ultimate goal. The ultimate goal in football is to win the game.

The same is true in our finances. The ultimate goal is to be an extravagant giver. In the process of saving and investing, our finances will be in order, and we will be out of debt. That is not the ultimate goal, it is simply a byproduct of our efforts.

John D. Rockefeller was the wealthiest man alive during his lifetime. He owned Standard Oil and had millions of dollars back in the 1800s. He went on to become the world's first billionaire in 1916.[1] Someone asked him how he became so wealthy, and he said that he follows the 10-10-80 principle.[2] In other words he gave away 10% of his income, he saved 10%, and then he lived off the other 80%. So here is the richest man alive at that time, and he credited his wealth to his giving.

The wealthiest man in the 20th century was Bill Gates. He accumulated over 60 billion dollars during his career at Microsoft. Instead of working into his 60s, he left Microsoft to start the Bill and Melinda Gates Foundation. This nonprofit organization now helps millions of people around the world. You see the ultimate goal for him is to give and help other people.

Warren Buffet is another billionaire. He accumulated great wealth through the companies that he owned and worked at. In his will he is leaving a majority of his fortune to charity.[3] His children are only getting a small portion of his estate. Why is that? Because he sees the ultimate goal of giving to help others is more important than leaving billions of dollars to a few children.

Giving not only benefits the person that receives the gift, but it also benefits the giver as well. When we give, we become less selfish and more generous people. Have you ever met someone who is really selfish and only thinks about themselves? Are they fun to be around? On the other hand, have you ever met someone who is really generous? Would you rather be friends with them? Generous people are happier people. They have more joy and fulfillment in their lives and tend to prosper in their relationships and their wealth.

How Much?

How much should people give? That is really up to you. Once you start giving you will see that it can be even more rewarding than spending money on yourself. You can give to your favorite charity, to a church, to family member in need, and even to a complete stranger. Think of giving like investing, but in the opposite direction. You can diversify your giving by giving to different organizations and individuals.

When we give, we are really just giving people a part of our life. For example, if you make $100 a day, and you give someone $200, it is like you are giving away two days of your life. So when we give of our finances, we are ultimately giving away part of our life. Jesus said that there is no greater love than to lay down one's life for his friends.[4] So giving financially is a way in which we can love others and help the world to be a better place.

Remember the purpose of this book is not to teach you how to stack up a large amount of money to hoard and keep for yourself. The real purpose is for you to be debt free and have some money saved so that you can help people when the need arises. Remember that giving is the real adventure. That is where the fun begins. Being debt free is good. Having money is great. But giving is grand. It is better than the first two combined. If you got excited at the thought of being debt free, then wait until you experience the joy of giving. It will take you to a whole "nother" level.

The best way to describe the joy of giving is through parenting. If you have children, you can probably relate to the joy it is to get your kids' gifts for their birthday or Christmas. For me, I don't get too excited about gifts on Christmas because I know that I can buy what I want throughout the year. However, my kids are different. They don't have a job that allows them to earn their own income yet. So when they get a gift, they get super excited. They're excited because they have no other way to get the gift that was purchased for them. Some women, my wife included, feel so strong about giving gifts to their children, that they would rather give something to their kids than get something for themselves.

The same is true when you begin to give. You will find people get super excited because often times they do not have the means to get the gift that you provide for them. When you begin to give like this, you will find it much more rewarding than receiving.

So let's work on getting an emergency fund. Let's work on getting the credit cards paid off. Let's work on saving and investing. But most importantly, let's be a part of the All-Star Team and work on giving and making a difference in this world. You can do this. You can win at the game of finances.

Questions for Study

1. What is the purpose of being debt free, saving, and investing?

2. What are the benefits of giving?

3. What are three things you have learned from this book that you want to implement in your life?

Appendix A

SPENDING PLAN WORKSHEET

Spending Plan Worksheet	
PART 1: MONTHLY INCOME	
Person 1: After Tax Monthly Income	
Person 2: After Tax Monthly Income	
Other Income	
Total Income	

PART 2: GIVING	
Charities	
Other Giving	
Total Giving and Charities	

PART 3: SAVINGS (10%)	
Saving for Emergencies	
Saving for Retirement (401K, IRA)	
Saving for Vacations, Education, and Other Goals	
Total Savings	

PART 4: DEBT (5%)	
Credit Cards	
Student Loans	
Other Debt (excluding car and home)	
Total Debt	

PART 5: HOUSING (35%)	
Mortgage/Rent	
Home/Renters Insurance	
Electric Bill	
Water Bill	
Natural Gas Bill	
Cable/Satellite TV	
Internet Access	
Phone/Mobile Phone Bill	
Repairs/Maintenance	
Other _____________	
Total Housing	

PART 6: TRANSPORTATION (15%)	
Car Payment(s)	
Car Insurance	
Gasoline	
Repairs/Maintenance	
Total Transportation	

PART 7: LIFE (25%)	
Groceries	
Going Out to Eat	
Entertainment	
Health Insurance	
Daycare	
Pet care	
Memberships (Gym, etc.)	
Clothes	
Other: ______________	
Other: ______________	
Other: ______________	
Total Life	

PART 8: RESULTS	
Total Monthly Income	
Total Monthly Expenses	
Under or (Over) Budget	

Appendix B

NET WORTH WORKSHEET

Net Worth Worksheet	
PART 1: WHAT I OWN	**Current Value**
Checking Accounts	
Savings Accounts	
Money Market Accounts	
Certificates of Deposits	
Stock/Bond/Mutual Funds	
Life Insurance (cash value)	
Residence (market value)	
Other Real Estate	
Car 1 Resale Value	
Car 2 Resale Value	
Other Personal Property	
IRAs/401Ks	
Other (Businesses, etc…)	
Total Assets	

PART 2: WHAT I OWE	% Rate	Current Balance
Mortgage		
Additional Real Estate Loans		
Car Loan		
Car Loan		
Credit Card		
Credit Card		
Credit Card		
School Loans		
Other (IRS, Medical, etc.)		
Total Debts		

PART 3: NET WORTH	
Total Assets	
Total Debts	
Net Worth	

Appendix C

LAST WILL AND TESTAMENT FORM

LAST WILL AND TESTAMENT

of

____

(Full Names and Surname)

____

(Identification / Social Security Number(s)

____

____

(Address)

1. Declaration

I hereby declare that this is my last will and testament and that I hereby revoke, cancel, and annul all wills and codicils previously made by me either jointly or severally. I declare that I am of legal age to make this will and of sound mind and that this last will and testament expresses my wishes without undue influence or duress.

2. Family Details

I am married to ______________________________ hereinafter referred to as my spouse.

I have the following children:

Name: ______________________ Date of Birth _________

Name: ______________________ Date of Birth _________

Name: ______________________ Date of Birth _________

3. Appointment of Executors

3.1. I hereby nominate, constitute and appoint ___________________________ as Executor or if this Executor is unable or unwilling to serve then I appoint ________________________ as alternate Executor.

3.2. I hereby give and grant the Executor all powers and authority as are required or allowed in law, and especially that of assumption.

3.3. I hereby direct that my Executors shall not be required to furnish security and shall serve without any bond.

3.4. Pending the distribution of my estate my Executors shall have authority to carry on any business, venture or partnership in which I may have any interest at the time of my death.

3.5. My Executors shall have full and absolute power in his/her discretion to sell all or any assets of my estate, whether by public auction or private sale and shall be entitled to let any property in my estate on such terms and conditions as may be acceptable to my beneficiaries.

3.6. My Executors shall have authority to borrow money for any purpose connected with the liquidation and administration of my estate and to that end may encumber any of the assets of my estate.

4. Guardian

4.1. Failing the survival of my spouse as natural guardian I appoint ______________________ or failing him / her I appoint ______________________ to be the legal Guardian of my minor children named:

______________________________ ______________________________

______________________________ ______________________________

until such time as they attain the age of ________ years.

4.2. I direct that my nominated Guardian shall not be required to furnish security for acting in that capacity.

5. Beneficiary

5.1 I bequeath the whole of my estate, property and effects, whether movable or immovable, wheresoever situated and of whatsoever nature (except as listed in 5.2) to my spouse ________________________.

5.2 I bequeath the greater of _____ % of the estate or the amount of $____________ and the following assets _____________________________ to the non-profit charity __________________________ from the estate.

6. Alternate Beneficiaries

6.1. Should my spouse not survive me by thirty (30) days I direct that the whole of my estate, property and effects, whether movable or immovable, wheresoever situated and of whatsoever nature be divided amongst my children named in 2. above in equal shares (after distributions listed in 5.2).

6.2. Should my said spouse and I and my children all die simultaneously or within thirty (30) days of each other as a result of the same accident or calamity, then and in that event, I direct that the whole of my estate, property and effects, whether movable or immovable, wheresoever situated and of whatsoever nature shall devolve as follows (after distributions listed in 5.2):

____

____

____

____

____

7. Special Requests

______ I direct that on my death my remains shall be buried at __________________________ and all funeral expenses shall be paid out of my estate.

OR

______ I direct that on my death my remains shall be cremated and all cremation expenses shall be paid out of my estate.

8. General

8.1. Words signifying one gender shall include the others and words signifying the singular shall include the plural and vice versa where appropriate.

8.2. Should any provision of this will be judged by an appropriate court of law as invalid it shall not affect any of the remaining provisions whatsoever.

Signed on this __________________ day of __________________20_____ at this location ____ in the presence of the undersigned witnesses.

SIGNED: ________________________________

WITNESSES

As witnesses we declare that we are of sound mind and of legal age to witness a will and that to the best of our knowledge ______________________, the creator of this will, is of legal age to make a will, appears to be of sound mind and signed this will willingly and free of undue influence or duress. We declare that he / she signed this will in our presence as we then signed as witnesses in his / her presence and in the presence of each other witness, all being present at the same time. Under penalty of perjury we declare these statements to be true and correct on this

_________________ day of __________________ 20 __

at this location _________________________________.

Witness 1.

Name: ____

Address: ____

Signature: ____

Witness 2.

Name:____

Address: ____

Signature: ____

ENDNOTES

Chapter 2

[1] Opdyke, Jeff D. "How to Make a Spending Plan." The Wall Street Journal, 3 Nov. 2008, www.wsj.com/articles/SB122548317028388819

[2] Sandomir, Richard. "Tyson's Bankruptcy Is a Lesson In Ways to Squander a Fortune." The New York Times, 5 Aug. 2003, www.nytimes.com/2003/08/05/sports/tyson-s-bankruptcy-is-a-lesson-in-ways-to-squander-a-fortune.html

Chapter 4

[1] Issa, Erin El. "2016 American Household Credit Card Debt Study." Nerdwallet, 3 Nov. 2008, www.nerdwallet.com/blog/credit-card-data/average-credit-card-debt-household

[2] Proverbs 22:7. NIV.

[3] Michon, Kathleen. "Texas Bankruptcy Exemptions." The Bankruptcy Site, 24 May 2016, www.thebankruptcysite.org/exemptions/texas.html#

Chapter 5

[1] "Depreciation Infographic: How Fast Does My New Car Lose Value?" Edmunds, 24 Sep. 2010, www.edmunds.com/car-buying/how-fast-does-my-new-car-lose-value-infographic.html

[2] "Extended Car Warranties: An Expensive Gamble." Consumer Reports, Feb. 2014, www.consumerreports.org/cro/magazine/2014/04/extended-warranties-for-cars-are-an-expensive-game/index.htm

[3] Whitfield, Fredricka. "Eating on a Dollar a Day." CNN, 23 Aug. 2010, www.youtube.com/watch?v=3VLoOiqJlrc

Chapter 6

[1] Katz, Sharon. "Defense Wins Championships: Consistently True." ESPN, 25 Jan. 2016, www.espn.com/blog/statsinfo/post/_/id/114053/defense-wins-championships-consistently-true

[2] "The Ten Countries Where People Save the Most Money." 24/7 Wall Street, 15 Aug. 2011, 247wallst.com/investing/2011/08/15/the-ten-countries-where-people-save-the-most-money/3/

[3] Hayashi, Fumio. "Why Is Japan's Saving Rate So Apparently High." NBER, 1986, www.nber.org/chapters/c4247.pdf

[4] Zumbrun, Josh. "Younger Generation Faces a Savings Deficit." The Wall Street Journal, 9 Nov. 2014, www.wsj.com/articles/savings-turn-negative-for-younger-generation-1415572405

[5] Scheer, Roddy and Moss, Doug. "Use It and Lose IT: The Outsize Effect of U.S. Consumption on the Environment." Scientific American, www.scientificamerican.com/article/american-consumption-habits/

[6] Proverbs 21:20 NLT

[7] Johnson, Angela. "76% of Americans are Living Paycheck-to-Paycheck." CNN Money, 24 Jun. 2013, money.cnn.com/2013/06/24/pf/emergency-savings/index.html

[8] "529 Plans: Questions and Answers." Internal Revenue Service, www.irs.gov/uac/529-plans-questions-and-answers

[9] "Coverdell Education Savings Accounts (ESA)." Internal Revenue Service, www.irs.gov/publications/p970/ch07.html#en_US_2015_publink1000178469

Chapter 7

[1] "Daily Treasury Yield Curve Rates." U.S. Department of the Treasury, www.treasury.gov/resource-center/data-chart-center/interest-rates/Pages/TextView.aspx?data=yield

[2] "Rule of 72." Money Chimp, www.moneychimp.com/features/rule72.htm

[3] "Historical CD Interest Rates – 1984-2016." Bankrate, 19 Apr. 2016, www.bankrate.com/finance/cd-rates-history-0112.aspx

[4] "US 20 Year Bond Yield." Trading Economics, 12 Feb. 2025, https://tradingeconomics.com/united-states/20-year-bond-yield

[5] "American Eagle Coins." U.S. Mint, catalog.usmint.gov/coin-programs/american-eagle-coins/

[6] Caporal, Jack. "Lottery Statistics and Revenue by State" Motley Fool Money, 12 Dec. 2024, https://www.fool.com/money/research/lottery-statistics/

[7] Rosenberg, Tina. "Playing the Odds on Saving." The New York Times, 15 Jan. 2014, opinionator.blogs.nytimes.com/2014/01/15/playing-the-odds-on-saving/?_r=0

Chapter 8

[1] Phipps, Jennie. "Keep the Mortgage or Pay Off the House?." Bankrate, www.bankrate.com/finance/mortgages/keep-the-mortgage-or-pay-off-the-house--1.aspx

Chapter 9

[1] Hellmich, Nanci. "One-Third Have Almost No Retirement Savings." USA Today, 21 Apr. 2015, www.usatoday.com/story/money/2015/04/21/no-retirement-savings/26070017/

[2] Proverbs 13:22

[3] "Ultimate Guide to Retirement." CNN Money, money.cnn.com/retirement/guide/insurance_life.moneymag/index9.htm

[4] Widness, Brett. "Ten Things You Should Know About Writing a Will." AARP, May 2012, www.aarp.org/money/estate-planning/info-09-2010/ten_things_you_should_know_about_writing_a_will.html

Chapter 10

[1] O'Donnell, Carl. "The Rockefellers: The Legacy of History's Richest Man." Forbes, 11 Jul. 2014, www.forbes.com/sites/carlodonnell/2014/07/11/the-rockefellers-the-legacy-of-historys-richest-man/#71c8f47560e7

[2] Peck, Joseph. "The 10-10-80 Principle." Your Daily Blessing, 13 Jul. 2016, yourdailyblessing.com/the-10-10-80-principle/

[3] Halpert, Julie. "Boomers Mimic Warren Buffett When it Comes to Inheritances." CNBC, 9 Mar. 2015, www.cnbc.com/2015/03/09/boomers-mimic-warren-buffett-when-it-comes-to-inheritances.html

[4] John 15:13 NIV.

www.ingramcontent.com/pod-product-compliance
Lightning Source LLC
LaVergne TN
LVHW022057200926
848481LV00003B/951
* 9 7 9 8 2 9 5 7 1 4 1 0 8 *